Wagner Moments

"Wagner gives expression to things which in the rest of us,
and in the rest of art, are unconscious because they are repressed.
This repression, this inner conflict, is inseparable from living,
and is part of the personality of each one of us. It is from, and to,
this level of personality that Wagner's music speaks."

Bryan Magee
Aspects of Wagner

Wagner Moments

A Celebration of Favorite Wagner Experiences

AMADEUS PRESS

An Imprint of Hal Leonard Corporation
New York

Due to space considerations, credits can be found on pp. 227–231, which should be considered an extension of the copyright page.

Published in 2007 by
Amadeus Press (an imprint of Hal Leonard Corporation)
512 Newark Pompton Turnpike
Pompton Plains, New Jersey 07444

Printed in the United States of America

Book design by Snow Creative Services

Library of Congress Cataloging-in-Publication Data is available upon request.

ISBN10: 1574671596
ISBN13: 9781574671599

www.amadeuspress.com

For Father Lee, and for Peter Allen

who, from that big cathedral in Lincoln Center,
have brought Wagner Moments to thousands.

And also for Hilary and Adams
who have given me moments better even than Wagner Moments.

Contents

Preface		xi
Acknowledgments		xiv
Introduction		xvii
1	Carolyn Abbate	1
2	Tim Albery	3
3	Peter Allen	5
4	Thomas Arthur	7
5	Margaret Atwood	9
6	W. H. Auden	11
7	Robert Bailey	13
8	Joe Banno	15
9	Daniel Barenboim	18
10	Charles Baudelaire	20
11	Michael Berger-Sandhofer	22
12	Lord Berners	24
13	Günter Blobel	27
14	Carol Ann Bogash	28
15	Richard Bradshaw	30
16	Frederick A. Buechner	32
17	Jeffrey Buller	34
18	Willa Cather	38
19	Paul Cézanne	40
20	Marcia Davenport	42
21	Harry de Wildt	44
22	Jonathan Dean	46
23	Achille-Claude Debussy	48
24	John Louis DiGaetani	51
25	Plácido Domingo	53
26	Les Dreyer	55
27	Leslie Dunton-Downer	56
28	T. S. Eliot	59
29	Kenneth R. Feinberg	62
30	Martin Feinstein	64

31	Aurelius Fernandez	66
32	Sherman Finger	68
33	Benjamin Foster	70
34	Peter Gelb	71
35	Raymond Geuss	73
36	Thomas Grey	77
37	Stuart Hamilton	80
38	Pamela Jones Harbour	82
39	Daniel Herwitz	84
40	Adams Holman	87
41	Marilyn Horne	89
42	Hans Hotter	91
43	Christine Hunter	93
44	Linda and Michael Hutcheon	95
45	Henry James	98
46	Speight Jenkins	100
47	James Joyce	102
48	Benjamin Kamins	104
49	Wassily Kandinsky	107
50	Alexandra Kauka	109
51	Winnie Klotz	110
52	Evelyn Lear	112
53	Father M. Owen Lee	115
54	Oscar Levant	117
55	Claude Lévi-Strauss	119
56	Bernard Levin	121
57	Michael Levine	124
58	C. S. Lewis	125
59	Jonathan Lewsey	128
60	Saul Lilienstein	131
61	George and Nora London	134
62	Laura Maioglio	136
63	Thomas Mann	138
64	Peter Mark	140
65	Thomas May	142
66	Richard Mayer	145
67	James McCourt	147
68	Barry Millington	148
69	Alisdair Neale	150
70	Ernest Newman	151
71	Friedrich Nietzsche	153

72 John Edward Niles   155
73 Ignacy Jan Paderewski   156
74 Tim Page   157
75 Jan Peerce   159
76 John Pohanka   161
77 Andrew Porter   162
77 Marcel Proust   163
79 Pierre-Auguste Renoir   165
80 La Revue Wagnérienne   168
81 Kenneth Ringle   171
82 Rudolph Sabor   173
83 John Singer Sargent and Judith Gautier   175
84 Christina Scheppelmann   176
85 Iain Scott   178
86 George Bernard Shaw and Alfred Turco   180
87 Beverly Sills   183
88 Georg Solti   184
89 Frederic Spotts   186
90 Jason Stearns   187
91 Thomas Stewart   189
92 Jeffery Swann   192
93 Roman Terleckyj   194
94 Anthony Tommasini   195
95 Arturo Toscanini   200
96 Astrid Varnay   202
97 Paul Verlaine   204
98 Shirley Verrett   206
99 Frederica von Stade   207
100 Stephen Wadsworth   209
101 Alan Wagner   211
102 Richard Wagner   213
103 John Ward   215
104 Michael Wiedman   217
105 Simon Williams   219
106 Virginia Woolf   221
107 Francesca Zambello   223

Epilogue   225
Sources and Permissions   227

Preface

I can lay my hand on the very moment.
—*C. S. Lewis*

A good deal of my adult life has been spent—however meager the results—trying to explain and to advocate the indispensable value of Wagner's art and to work for the expansion of the Wagner audience. This book is another attempt in that regard.

As always with Wagner, the exertions of both explanation and advocacy are bipolar, if not contradictory. On one hand, Wagner needs to be, and in fact is becoming, "normalized." I have written elsewhere that since World War II Wagner's operas—music dramas, if you insist—have been performed in increasing numbers, and in new places.[1] And they have been relentlessly, and happily, escaping two dark shadows: of Wagner the man and Wagner the essayist. Wagner's art deserves to stand on its own, experienced by audiences for its inherent qualities, unaffected by the kind of man Wagner (supposedly) was or the twelve volumes of prose that he wrote.

On the other hand, and despite the reasonable proposition that we should be *listening* to the operas, letting them speak for themselves, people like me, and people much wiser, keep writing, not only abut the operas, but about the artist, the extraordinary life he lived, the insightful and repellent things he wrote, his pervasive influences, and what his operas "really mean." A few even write about Wagner's music![2]

And we keep trying to describe, to put into words, what Wagner's operas have meant to our personal lives. C. S. Lewis offers an eloquent contribution to this volume; the memory of his Wagner Moment was still vivid when he wrote his autobiography many years after the event. Yet he is by no means unique, for Wagner—arguably as much as any

---

1. See "The Golden *Ring* in a Golden Age," from *Inside the Ring*, edited by John DiGaetani (2006).

2. See Wagner Moment 94 by the *New York Times* critic Anthony Tommasini.

artist—affects us, has an *impact* on us. For many people over the past century and a half, Wagner has provided epiphanies and awakenings, nothing less than a window on the nature of the outside world, and a mirror into our interior lives.

Verbalizing the ineffable may be an impossible task, but it is hardly a futile one, as I think the contributors to this book demonstrate.

This collection provides some remarkable convergences. It is striking, for example, that so many Wagner Moments have come to adolescent males at the age (more or less) of thirteen. As writer and director Jonathan Lewsey writes in his entry (see Wagner Moment 59): "Bernard Shaw identified the age of thirteen as being the birth of moral passion." That may be as good an explanation as any why nearly twenty contributors, including Lewsey and Shaw, were struck by Wagner at that impressionable and vulnerable, but resolute and heroic age.

Many contributors have been stunned when, on first hearing Wagner's music, it is as if they had heard it before. Charles Baudelaire was one, and as the concert pianist Jeffrey Swann writes (see Wagner Moment 92), on hearing just the first measure of the *Tristan* Prelude: "the power of the moment was not so much that I felt like I was discovering something new, on the outside, but that I was recognizing something that had been there all along on the inside, and that it was becoming manifest." Somehow, Wagner reveals us to ourselves.

On a prosaic note, and for those keeping score, a moderately accurate tally of operas among the forty or so specifically cited in this book breaks down like this:

> *The Flying Dutchman*: 2
> *Tannhäuser*: 7
> *Lohengrin*: 4
> *Tristan und Isolde*: 7
> *Die Meistersinger von Nürnberg*: 3
> *Das Rheingold*: 3
> *Die Walküre*: 10
> *Siegfried*: 1
> *Götterdämmerung*: 2
> *Der Ring des Nibelungen*: 3
> *Parsifal*: 4

But one can't end prosaically when talking about Wagner Moments. So I turn, as I always should, to Father Lee, whose prose comes as close as we are likely to get to the ineffable poetry of Wagner's music:

> The intuitive Wagner saw deeper into human nature than the rest of us are likely to do. And so we need him, the wounded Philoctetes with the God-given power to see unerringly into ourselves and so to help us with our lives.[3]

---

3. *Wagner: The Terrible Man and his Truthful Art* (1999).

Acknowledgments

The idea for this book—as for most of what I do—came from Mrs. Holman, my partner of more than forty years. A successful author in her own right and filled with Wagner Moments of her own, she suggested that a collected volume might be entertaining, even enlightening. For her guidance in this, as in so much else, I am grateful.

The regular practice of eliciting Wagner Moments comes from the Wagner Society of Washington, D.C., which it has been my privilege to chair during the nine years of its existence. One of that society's activities has been a monthly lecture, after which it has been our custom to take our speaker to a Chinese dinner and ask for his or her Wagner Moment—that "aha!" moment when one first connected with Wagner, became hooked on Wagner, possibly in a way that was to have consequences.

Many Wagner Moments are indeed epiphanic, though certainly not all. Some of our speakers have had no Wagner Moments at all. Some became Wagnerians over an extended period. And some Moments are subjects of mirth more than transcendence. Nevertheless, I am grateful to my colleagues at the Wagner Society for providing these opportunities.

All of the contributors to this volume—at least those who are still alive—have had to endure my asking them to take time from busy lives to provide their Wagner Moments. This has involved, from time to time, a certain level of nagging of which I am not proud. So, to them, who truly *are* this book, I extend both my thanks and my apologies.

And I think none of them will be offended if I relate one little story about these responses. I first sent out a batch of Moment requests in June 2005, including one to Plácido Domingo. Most people are aware that Domingo is widely recognized as the "busiest man in the world," and at the time he was singing somewhere in Europe. Nevertheless, here comes Domingo's Wagner Moment—the very next day, typed and signed by himself. I think readers will agree that Domingo's Moment is especially powerful.

What I owe Father Owen Lee I cannot write here. So I will limit my remarks to his contribution to this book. In addition to his magnificent introduction, and his encyclopedic knowledge of so many who have been changed by Wagner (no wonder nobody wanted to go up against Father Lee on the Texaco Quiz!), he has been a genuine collaborator in this exercise. It was Father Lee who made me brave enough to write my first poor book, on Wagner's *Ring*, and I could never have persevered with this one, or made it better, without his continuing guidance and inspiring support. Father Lee is passionate, informed, articulate, and expert in matters Wagnerian, not to mention music in general—his latest book for Amadeus Press is *The Great Instrumental Works*. But it does stagger the mind to think that these achievements are exceeded by perhaps even greater passions and expertise—certainly for his calling as priest, but also for teaching, for writing on Virgil, Horace, and the Greeks—and for Jerome Kern and Richard Rodgers. Can there have been a fuller life?

Special thanks, too, to Iain Scott, Saul Lilienstein, and Carolyn Abbate, three of our best Wagner analysts. Iain always coats his insights with disarming common sense; I think this has something to do with the innate good manners of Canadians, but his modesty really can't obscure his brilliance. In any case, Iain has, in addition to contributing his own Moment and a gaggle of good advice, rounded up the Canadians' Wagner Moments in this volume.

Saul has always been there for me, to answer questions and fill in at least some of my many musical and other gaps—whether acquainting me with Chabrier's "Souvenirs of Bayreuth" or Verlaine's "Parsifal." Saul knows, too, that the Prelude to the *Meistersinger's* third act comes from somewhere deep in Richard Wagner.

I have frequently referred to Carolyn Abbate as Princeton's "beautiful mind," but now she has moved to Harvard. Her work is graceful, elegant, original, but also, on Wagner, wary if not appropriately skeptical, and I hope I have learned much from her.

Chris Boutlier has been of invaluable help as editor, proofreader, printer, computer guru, and formatter. He has with unending patience turned my scribblings into a manuscript fit for the publisher.

As for the publishers, I am deeply indebted to John Cerullo, Carol Flannery, and Gail Siragusa of Amadeus Press. I had assumed that after my *Wagner's Ring* book, Amadeus would have had enough of me. But John and I had talked long ago about a Wagner Moments book, and he gave an immediate and unqualified green light to the project. As for Carol and Gail, I can't imagine an easier collaboration between author, editor, and publisher.

Introduction

Father M. Owen Lee

Wagner Moments! Everyone who listens to music has had at least one of them. For some, such as André Gide, the Wagner Moment was one of "passionate aversion." For others, such as the young C. S. Lewis, it was an epiphany—as if "the sky had turned round." Some of the least likely people have been powerfully moved by Wagner. Theodor Herzl, the founder of modern political Zionism, was prompted by a performance of *Tannhäuser* to write his manifesto, "The Jewish State." One of the disciples of Dorothy Day, the radical New York social worker, was astonished to find her moved to tears by a Saturday afternoon Wagner broadcast. At the college where I have spent my life teaching, the eminent historian of philosophy Étienne Gilson once wept openly in the midst of a lecture at the mere thought of *Parsifal* and said that nothing in art meant more to him than its hero's purity, steadfastness, and compassion for the suffering of others. "It is the greatest of operas," he told me. "The highest in the heaven of heavens."

The famous composers of the past may not have described their Wagner moments in detail, but we have any number of brief responses in which they tell of being profoundly affected by such moments. Anton Bruckner used to sit at Bayreuth with his eyes closed, ignoring the stage action (which he did not even attempt to understand), totally immersed in the music. He dedicated his third symphony to Wagner and wrote perhaps his greatest music, the Adagio of his Seventh Symphony, as another tribute. He once sank to his knees to kiss Wagner's hand and say, "O, Master, I worship you." (Wagner rewarded the worship with "There, there, Bruckner. Good night!")

For many composers, the transcendent Wagner moment came at a performance of *Parsifal*. Max Reger wrote: "When I first heard *Parsifal* at Bayreuth, I cried for two weeks. Then I became a musician." And Gustav Mahler, hearing *Parsifal*, recorded, "When I came out of the Festspielhaus I realized that I had undergone the greatest and most soul-searching experience of my life, and that I would carry that experience with me for the rest of my days." Hugo Wolf, again after *Parsifal*, stumbled out of the theater and sat by himself for hours with his head buried in his hands; he wrote of the experience that "This is without doubt the most beautiful and sublime work in the whole field of art. My whole being reels in the perfect world of this wonderful work, as if in some blissful ecstasy. I could die even now." *Parsifal* evoked a similar reaction from the Scandinavian Jean Sibelius. "Nothing in the world has made so overwhelming an impression on me. All my innermost heartstrings throbbed." Edvard Grieg attended the Bayreuth premiere of *The Ring* and wrote: "Yesterday I came face to face with the greatest that the music drama of the century has given us. I can now understand Liszt's assessment of the great Wagner when he says it rises above all our epoch's art like Mont Blanc over the Alps."

French composers were not immune either. After hearing *Tristan*, Chabrier resigned from his government post and took up composing; after he heard *Parsifal* he wrote, "Never in all my life have I had an artistic experience at all comparable to this. It is overwhelming. One comes out after each act (I do at least) absolutely overcome, bewildered, distraught, with tears running down one's cheeks." Charles Gounod prayed, after the disastrous Paris premiere of *Tannhäuser*, "May God give me a failure like that." And Jules Massenet wrote, "So overwhelming is the power of Wagner that after hearing one of his works you vow never to compose again. Then you forget a little and start anew." Debussy might have hated the passionate overstatement of the frenzied characters in *Parsifal*, but he was profoundly affected by the stained-glass transparency of its orchestration and declared it "one of the most beautiful monuments raised to the imperishable glory of music." *Parsifal* echoes throughout his *Pelléas et Mélisande*.

The Klingsor of Bayreuth cast a spell over the Italians as well, however much they tried to resist. Verdi sent for Wagner's scores and (though it was once *de rigeur* to deny this) studied them: there are lessons learned from *Lohengrin* in *Aida*, from *Parsifal* in *Otello*, from *Meistersinger* in *Falstaff*. And the maestro of Sant' Agatha told an interviewer that he stood "in wonder and terror" before *Tristan*: when Wagner died, Verdi knowingly wrote, "Triste, triste, triste." As for the maestro of Torre del Lago, Puccini had, in his bohemian days, saved his pennies to buy the score of *Parsifal* and, struggling at the end his intractable *Turandot*, took a brief look at *Tristan*, only to say ruefully, "What are the rest of us but mere mandolin strummers? This tremendous music destroys us. It makes us incapable of composing any more."

The rivalry between Wagner and Brahms was never so bitter as the supporters of each made it appear. One of the great symphonist's doctors reported, "I never called at Brahms's home without finding one or another of Wagner's scores lying open on the piano. He once spontaneously told me that he would have liked to have gone to Bayreuth if he had not feared that capital would be made out of his presence there." Asked near the end why he never wrote an opera, Brahms said, "After Wagner it was impossible."

That Brahmsian among American songwriters, Jerome Kern, used to keep a little bust of Wagner on his piano and when he wasn't satisfied with what he was writing would turn it to the wall, saying, "Wagner doesn't like it." And more recently, when Georg Solti called on Richard Strauss to discuss orchestral details in *Der Rosenkavalier*, Strauss drew from the shelf his score of *Tristan*, a score he always conducted from memory, and said, "Let's talk about this!"

Of course there were composers who were not happy about the Wagner phenomenon. Some made witty responses: Rossini, asked by Auber how he had liked *Tannhäuser*, replied, "You have to hear it more than once—and I'm not going back." Balakirev said, "After *Lohengrin* I had a splitting headache, and all through the night I dreamed about a goose." Stravinsky recorded, after his experience at Bayreuth, "I sat humble and motionless, but at the end of a quarter of an hour I could not bear any more. Crack! Now I had done it! My chair had creaked, making a noise that brought on me the furious scowls of a hundred pairs of eyes."

There were also shocked responses. The pious César Franck wrote "Poison!" across his score of *Tristan*—though he kept it handy and learned more than one lesson from it. Tchaikovsky, attending the first *Ring* cycle at Bayreuth, exclaimed, "What really astounds me is the seriousness with which this philosophizing German sets the most inane subjects to music." He wrote to his brother Modest, "After the last note I felt as though I had been let out of prison." He thought *Tristan* "an endless void, without movement, without life," and he could not understand how, despite its "wealth of harmony," anyone could listen "without laughter or without being bored" to *Parsifal*. All the same, when he penned his own main melody for *Swan Lake*, Tchaikovsky remembered the recurrent "question" motif first sung by Lohengrin, the swan knight, to the maidenly Elsa. "*Lohengrin*," he said, "will always be the crown of all his works." Tchaikovsky may not have admitted it, but it seems clear that he had had his Wagner moment—early on.

In the remarkable book you have in your hand, J. K. Holman, author of *Wagner's* Ring: *A Listener's Companion and Concordance*, has assembled the Wagner Moments of many more celebrated people—some of them musicians, a number of them from other walks of life, some living, some no longer with us. It is a great pleasure for me to introduce this volume. On its pages you will renew your acquaintance with men and women you may never till now have known as fellow travelers, but who, like you, have caught sight of the Grail and felt its life-affirming power. Happy reading!

Wagner Moments

1

Carolyn Abbate

Carolyn Abbate, Fanny Peabody Professor of Music at Harvard University, is a wide-ranging humanist who ranks among the world's foremost authorities on opera. Spanning operas from Monteverdi to Ravel as well as film music and sound technology, Abbate's work crosses disciplinary boundaries from music into literature and philosophy. She is the author of In Search of Opera *and* Unsung Voices *and coauthor of the forthcoming* Penguin History of Opera. *She is also the translator of many French scholarly works. She was the recipient of a Guggenheim Fellowship in 1995 and National Endowment for the Humanities Fellowships in 1986 and 1994, and was awarded the Dent Medal of the Royal Music Association in 1993.*

During the late 1970s and early 1980s, through the good graces of Marcia Lazer and Joseph Clark—two friends working at the Metropolitan Opera—I was able to escape Princeton, New Jersey (where I was a student), and see operas virtually all the time, for free. Met employees could get passes for standing at the back of the dress circle during performances; there was no official standing room, just a few random uncomfortable perches. I still remember that the tickets for these spots resembled the normal tickets only in their size and design: rather than being printed on emerald or ruby or shiny gold stock, they were a fibrous gray as if made of recycled cardboard. One such *passepartout* put me there in December 1977 for the premiere of a new production of *Tannhäuser* conducted by James Levine, with James McCracken, Leonie Rysanek, and Grace Bumbry, and with the debuts of Bernd Weikl as Wolfram and Kathleen Battle as the little shepherd.

In some sense the whole performance was a Wagner Moment; in my memory it exists as an instance of rare perfection producing a kind of perpetual awe. Yet I also know that it was not some high point or intense melodrama, involving the full orchestra and the voices of Rysanek or McCracken, but rather a bagatelle that engendered the most powerful suspension of time: Battle's beautiful half-child, half-woman voice singing unaccompanied in Act I, scene 3, in the shepherd's song. No orchestra—no Wagnerian gravitas, no Wagnerian loudspeaker broadcasting at full volume, simply a single human sound filling the acoustic void. I also remember that this transfigured sound was brought forward, as it were. In the final scene, just after Tannhäuser dies, the young pilgrims return from Rome with a little boy at their head carrying the staff that has miraculously bloomed with green. On this night, the boy was looking at the staff with pure wonder and terror, as if he had seen something that he cannot describe but that has taken him to another planet—and he was singing along with the others, but his voice carried over everyone else's not by virtue of a separate or higher line, but for its unique grain and beauty, since the boy was Kathleen Battle reappearing incognito in the chorus. Her timbre became a leitmotif that existed apart from the score, an ephemeral leitmotif, you could say. Deciding what someone "meant" by bringing the shepherd's voice back without permission from Wagner's libretto or score seemed an unimportant matter, for my astonishment at the fortuitous power and mystery of that moment seemed as great as the wonder written on the little shepherd's face.

I ended up writing a tedious dissertation on *Tannhäuser*, feeling like a cat that leaves offerings of unlucky mice at the door of something very large and a little terrifying.

2

Tim Albery

Tim Albery, an Englishman who lives in Canada, is one of the world's best and busiest directors of theater and opera. His acclaimed production of the Ring *cycle for Scottish Opera, conducted by Sir Richard Armstrong and designed by Hildegard Bechtler and Ana Jebens, was presented at the Edinburgh Festival over four years, with the full cycle premiering in August 2003. It was also performed in Glasgow and Manchester.*

The summer of 2001 was probably a little late to be having a moment of epiphany with Wagner, given that I was directing the second part of the *Ring* cycle at the time for Scottish Opera.

Its cause was the scene between Wotan and Brünnhilde in Act II of *Die Walküre*, often thought of as a long retelling of the story so far by Wotan, beautiful but essentially undramatic. Working on this scene in the rehearsal room, two performers, a chair, a bed, and a bottle of scotch (a prop, not a directing aid), my residual fear of *The Ring* as a treacherous mountain to climb evaporated.

Das Rheingold had been fun the year before, a mad cartoon that speeds on its exuberant way to the final act of vanity that is the gods' entrance into Valhalla. *Die Walküre* was something different, a more daunting challenge. But start to do the work, and it reveals itself moment by moment as theater, as dramatic as anything in Ibsen.

The "Wotan and Brünnhilde" scene is not the narrative monologue that at first glance it may seem. Although Brünnhilde rarely has an interjection of more than a few words, the scene is rather an unraveling of a hitherto almost suffocatingly close father-and-favorite-daughter relationship (or, if we prefer, of the relationship between Wotan's ego and his will); it is a study of something little less than the nervous breakdown of the leader of the world, which forces Brünnhilde to realize that she will have to undertake for the first time an autonomous, self-willed action in defiance of her father. It is ultimately the springboard that will lead her by the end of the opera to actively embrace the possibility of a new life as a human being with free will, and all the terrors that implies.

The scene becomes a colossal duet of the struggle between the public and the private, of that point at which emotional need and political necessity meet, as compelling in its very different way as, say, the great duet between King Philip and Posa in Verdi's *Don Carlos*.

At some point during the first rehearsal of the scene was the moment that can maybe be best described as a kind of exhilarated relief: the realization that a six-year conversation with *The Ring* would be sustainable and fruitful, that Wagner, after the relative dramatic naiveties of the earlier operas, had become a great playwright and not just a great composer.

Editor's note: For more on the Wotan monologue, see Wagner Moment 42: Hans Hotter.

3

Peter Allen

In January 1975, at the culmination of a long career as actor, announcer, and narrator in radio, film, and television, Peter Allen was chosen for "the best job in classical music radio—really, the best job in the world":—host of the live Texaco Metropolitan Opera Saturday matinee radio broadcasts. In 1977 he announced the first of many "Live from the Met" telecasts, including the afternoon and evening gala performances celebrating the Met centennial in 1983.

Among his other assignments has been the long-running Opera House *program on New York's leading classical music radio station and the radio station of* The New York Times, *WQXR, where he was a staff announcer for many years.*

In 1988, for the Met Opera Guild, he wrote and narrated Talking about The Ring, *a series of highly praised cassettes about the four operas in Wagner's* Ring des Nibelungen *cycle, and since then has written and narrated* Talking about La Traviata.

He has narrated well over one hundred films, many of them prizewinning, including Light in the Window, *about the art of Vermeer, a short subject that won an Oscar.*

Like many in the industry, Allen came to radio by happy accident. While a sophomore English major at the Ohio State University, where he graduated Phi Beta Kappa, he was engaged by the university radio station as violist in a string quartet. But the other members of the quartet failed to materialize, and because he had acted on campus and in summer stock, he was assigned to performing in radio dramas, and his career was launched.

In addition to his extraordinary contribution to the cultural life of New York and a worldwide radio audience, Allen is best known to his many friends for his unfailing good humor and gentle courtesy.

My Wagner Moment was not a moment but a season. I had long enjoyed much Wagner, including parts of the *Ring* cycle, but, curiously, it was not until the season of 1974–75—my first season of announcing the broadcasts, beginning in January 1975—that I heard a complete cycle. I heard each of the operas at least five times, including rehearsals, but I was terribly, terribly disappointed not to be able to attend my seventh *Götterdämmerung* that season. It was then that I decided to do something to help others enjoy *The Ring*. I later went to Munich and enjoyed their spaceship version, in spite of the spaceship, and on my return to New York was pleasantly surprised to be asked to do a cassette introduction to *The Ring*. Come to think of it, now, as I write, it has become clear that the two years of writing and then recording *Talking about* The Ring were, after all, my extended Wagner Moment. They were an intense, glorious two years. Working on *The Ring* was among the most satisfying experiences of my life.

4

Thomas Arthur

Thomas Arthur is a lifelong amateur musician and music lover. Since retiring from the U.S. Office of Management and Budget, Tom and his wife, Yoko, have traveled the world to hear good music—especially Wagner. The Arthurs live in Washington, where they actively support choral, opera, and concert groups.

I grew up in what the world calls a village but what Texans call a little country town. There was plenty of music there in the schools, churches, and homes. More important, famous artists performed in recital on the stages of larger towns nearby. However, there were no great musical events there, and I had to wait until I was twenty to hear the Metropolitan Opera on tour in Dallas, 100 miles away.

Although I had owned opera recordings from the age of twelve, I had to await a larger family home to have a room of my own away from bothersome younger brothers with whom I had been sharing. Only then could I also have my own radio. It came as a birthday present when I turned fifteen—a $12.95 Silvertone from Sears. With it I was set to listen in privacy. Listening included the Met Saturday broadcasts, no matter how long they lasted! And listen I did. The first time I heard *Die Meistersinger von Nürnberg* was a contest with myself: could I listen to anything that lasted until six o'clock? I did. I made it to the end of *Die Meistersinger* but without a Wagner Moment to grab me. That had to wait until I was about seventeen and listening to a Met broadcast of *Tannhäuser*.

Some of the famous *Tannhäuser* melodies, its "greatest hits," were already familiar to me and everyone else back then, even to the point of boredom. The overture was a popular concert piece. The "Song to the Evening Star," "Elizabeth's Prayer," and the booming "Pilgrims' Chorus" were all familiar in piano transcriptions, some of which I had played. But the first time I heard Act III of *Tannhäuser* on my Silvertone, the sound of the mighty men of the Met chorus sent something through that three-inch speaker that I had not heard in those piano transcriptions—because it was not there! At the end of the "Pilgrims' Chorus" that afternoon, young Tommy was grabbed by the fortissimo "Hallelujah in Ewigkeit!" that the pilgrims sing twice before shuffling off on their way home. Wagner had made sure its repetition would affect us more by moderating the orchestral accompaniment when the chorus sings this great "Hallelujah" for the second time.

Now here was something truly new and different, and I ran to the music cabinet to find that wonderful "Hallelujah." Sure enough, it was not there in the piano transcriptions I had known, but I found it in a book of organ transcriptions I sometimes played from. I ran to the church, pulled out all of the stops on its organ, played that great piece, and let that wonderful "Hallelujah" thrill me over and over.

It has thrilled me many times since and is my favorite moment in any presentation of *Tannhäuser*. Since then, I've been able to let it move me in some of the world's best places to hear great Wagner singing—the Metropolitan, Bayreuth, the Dresden Semperoper, and others. But for that Silvertone on that Saturday afternoon, I might not have learned to really love the great music of Richard Wagner, and I am forever thankful for the radio and to the Met broadcast and—of course!—to Richard Wagner for giving me that and his passionate, sweeping beautiful music dramas. *Hallelujah in Ewigkeit!*

5

Margaret Atwood

Margaret Atwood is the author of more than forty books of fiction, poetry, and critical essays. Her most recent book, The Tent, *a collection of mini-fictions, was published by Nan A. Talese/Doubleday. Her novel* Oryx and Crake *was short-listed for the Man Booker Prize and the Giller Prize in Canada. Her other works include the 2000 Booker Prize–winning book* The Blind Assassin; Alias Grace, *which won the Giller Prize in Canada and the Premio* Mondello in Italy; The Robber Bride; Cat's Eye; The Handmaid's Tale; *and* The Penelopiad. *Atwood lives in Toronto with the writer Graeme Gibson.*

I used to dislike Wagner. That's putting it mildly: I used to *violently* dislike Wagner. The man was an egomaniacal monster, though among those who've made a big mark in any art he's not alone. Then there was the aura of virulent anti-Semitism associated with the name, helped on by Hitler's adulation. But also there was the Bugs Bunny cartoon version, with Bugs and Elmer Fudd chasing each other around wearing horned helmets and Teutonic pigtails. It's easy to poke fun at opera, and Wagnerian opera has had more fun poked at it than any other kind. The tendency to giggle can undercut the intended effect.

In addition to that, I somehow couldn't *hear* Wagner. I was on the side of Stravinsky, who said, "If you listen to *Parsifal* you will hear many disagreeable sounds." I could deal with "The Ride of the Valkyries," despite its use as militaristic helicopter music in the film *Apocalypse Now*, and some of *Lohengrin*, and the sea-storm music from *The Flying Dutchman*, but that was about all.

Then I had a conversion experience, right in Toronto's Hummingbird Centre: I went to the Canadian Opera Company production of *Die Walküre* in 2004. This was the first step in the COC's plan to stage each of the four operas in the gigantic *Ring* cycle separately and then present them in the fall of 2006, in sequence, as the opening fireworks act for the new see-everything, hear-everything Four Seasons Opera House.

I went in a skeptic and longtime Wagner-disliker and came out a big-eyed, weak-kneed wow-sayer. Not all of this was due to Wagner him- or itself. It was the production values. What fantastic sets and costumes! (By production designer Michael Levine.) What direction! (By Atom Egoyan, though each of the four *Ring* operas had a different director.) What musical mastery! (In the tussle between score and conductor, Bradshaw had won.) Aha! So that was what all the fuss was about! I finally got it!

6

W. H. Auden

Widely considered the greatest English poet of the twentieth century, Wystan Hugh Auden (1907–1973) was a prolific writer, a noted playwright, editor, essayist—and opera librettist. His first collection, Poems, *was published in 1930, and established him as the leading voice of a new generation. He wrote with astonishing technical virtuosity, in all manners of styles, and on subjects ranging from socialism and Freudian analysis to modern Protestant theology.*

The following excerpt is from Auden, *by Richard Davenport-Hines (1995).*

It was his mother whom he would not treat as an ordinary human being. It was her mythic influence that became almost an obsession. He identified "landscape" with the maternal body, and elaborated great symbolic roles for all mothers; yet Constance Auden's concrete influences were great enough. Pre-eminently these were musical and religious. When he was eight, she taught Wystan the words and music of the "love-potion" scene in Wagner's *Tristan und Isolde*, which mother and son would sing together, "Wystan taking the part of Isolde," as his brother John recalled, "with implications of which she was evidently totally unaware."

This must have been a scene of lovely tenderness at the time, although those who think too much about the "causes" of male homosexuality fasten a more narrow and dismal meaning on it. Wagnerian love duets were an intense and demanding exaction by a mother on a small boy, but they were the early making of a great librettist: the sort of experience that raises a sensitive child out of the pleasant, facile creativity of a cultivated amateur into the disciplined power that creates enduring compositions.

7

Robert Bailey

Robert Bailey is Carroll and Milton Petrie Professor of Music at New York University. During his long and distinguished career, he has pioneered the study in America of nineteenth-century and twentieth-century German music, and especially Wagner's music. In 1984 he edited Richard Wagner: Prelude and Transfiguration from *Tristan and Isolde. Bailey's legacy is additionally enhanced by his teaching and inspiring other significant American musical scholars, including Carolyn Abbate (see Wagner Moment 1).*

My first encounter with Wagner's music came quite early in my life—junior high school years—when I acquired a two-LP set of Toscanini's recordings of instrumental selections, and then a couple of years later when I acquired the piano/vocal scores of *Die Meistersinger* and checked out the complete score from the Flint Public Library.

When I was an undergraduate at Dartmouth, I came casually to know *Tristan* and *Die Walküre* and saw all of the operas except *Die Meistersinger* and *Parsifal*, which I saw in Munich when I studied piano there in 1959–1960.

I got to know the operas in greater depth during my graduate study in Princeton and decided I wanted to do my dissertation on some aspect of Wagner. The real epiphany came when I went to Bayreuth in the summer of 1963. Hoping to gain access to the Wagner family archives and to find a dissertation subject, I traveled to Bayreuth by train from Munich on June 17. I arrived in the late afternoon and checked into a hotel right across the plaza from the railway station. I had forgotten that June 17 was a West German holiday, so most everything in the town was closed, and a wonderful silence hung over the town. There was nothing to do, so I decided to walk up to the Festspielhaus, and that was when I experienced a real epiphany.

The sun was setting, and the air was permeated with the scent of the *Flieder* (elder), just as Sachs describes in Act II. As I walked up the Green Hill to the Festspielhaus, the sounds of the "Wach' auf" chorus came filtering down through the trees—Wilhelm Pitz was conducting a choral rehearsal as part of the preparations for Wieland Wagner's new production of the opera.

I have never forgotten that utterly magical half-hour—it will go with me to my grave. I knew then, with no further doubt, that I had found a spiritual home with Wagner's works and his Festspielhaus.

As a postscript, I can append the fact that my experience with *Die Meistersinger* in Bayreuth was intensified the following November. I had managed to get tickets for the Metropolitan Opera's Saturday matinee of the opera, a couple of days before which President John F. Kennedy was assassinated. Rudolf Bing walked out before the performance began and announced that since this particular opera was singularly appropriate for such an occasion, the performance would be dedicated to the memory of our martyred hero.

8

Joe Banno

Joe Banno has directed over fifty theatrical productions, including plays at Source Theatre Company (where he has served as artistic director since 1997), Folger Elizabethan Theatre, Washington Shakespeare Company, and theaters around the United States His directing work in opera and musical theatre has been seen in over thirty productions with a dozen companies, most recently at Wolf Trap Opera, Summer Opera Theatre Company, and the Alba Music Festival in northern Italy. As a director, he has received the Helen Hayes Award, the Mary Goldwater Award, and the Bud Yorkin Award. A frequent guest lecturer, conference panelist, competition judge, and acting coach, Banno has also managed a classical radio station, directed a new-works initiative at Opera America, and headed numerous workshops to develop new plays. He currently complements his stage-directing work with a second career as a music writer, serving as a classical reviewer for The Washington Post *(since 1993) and opera critic for the* Washington City Paper *(since 1989), as well as contributing freelance pieces to other publications.*

During my middle-school years, I attended a rather offbeat summer camp, held on the verdant grounds of a local private high school. Part arts camp, part progressive school, part egghead commune, it was designed to keep intellectually curious, culture-hungry kids firing on all synapses during the hot months. Among the dizzying array of electives on offer—what other summer camp lets a kid create a day of filmmaking, fencing, stock trading, jujitsu, and frog dissection?—was a session simply entitled "Opera."

What "Opera" entailed was stretching out on one of the cool slate tables in the school's science lab, being handed a Schirmer libretto, and listening to a recording of that week's chosen complete opera piping out of an old Crosley phonograph mounted on a cart. The man choosing the recordings was a chemistry teacher who sported all the affects of the classic nerd—spiky flattop, horn-rims, pocket protector, and Bermuda shorts worn with black socks and dress shoes. But he was a brainy character, with an unexpected tough-guy swagger and a martini-dry sense of humor. And he had absolutely no doubt in his mind that opera was the coolest music on earth.

I hadn't been tempted by *The Barber of Seville* or *Carmen* when their strains were wafting from the science lab—my curiosity about opera was always dampened when the music sounded too light, self-consciously tuneful, or easy on the ear. But I found myself popping my head in when *The Flying Dutchman* was being dusted off and placed on the turntable. Wagner seemed like just the place to dive into the art form, especially when that chemistry teacher mentioned the difficulty some people had with Wagner's "heaviness," "complexity," and "overwhelming impact." This I had to hear!

I was all of twelve at the time and loved the music of Elvis Presley, the Beatles, Richard Rodgers, and Beethoven in roughly equal measure. My passion for theater had been kindled by a slew of summer-stock musicals and an early exposure to Shakespeare, and thanks to PBS I had blossomed into a pint-sized classic-cinema buff. I suppose I brought all of those cultural first-loves into the science lab that afternoon. But nothing I knew could have prepared me for the moment that score started to thunder from the stereo.

It was a case of instant addiction: this stuff was like crack! The baleful brass figures, the ocean-swept coloration in the string writing, the romantic ache and psychological layering in the Dutchman's words, the seductive lyricism in the duets for Erik and Senta, the sheer compulsive drive of the text and the score—I had never heard anything so thrilling, so mesmerizing. I remember thinking even then (years before reading that it was Wagner's intention all along) that this was the perfect melding of Beethoven's power and Shakespeare's eloquence. What could be better than that?

The recording was the EMI set conducted by Franz Konwitschny, stark and tragically inflected, with a cast so vivid in their characterizations they truly seemed to leap from the speakers. (The word pointing of Dietrich Fischer-Dieskau's Dutchman and that arrestingly swarthy tone of Gottlob Frick's Daland have yet to be equaled.) The recording remains my gold standard for the work, and one that still transports me back to the instant I discovered Richard Wagner—then and now, the composer who touches a deeper place in me than any other.

9

Daniel Barenboim

Daniel Barenboim continues to expand a musical life that began to astonish people—including Wilhelm Furtwängler—when he was a child. As concert pianist, chamber musician, and conductor, he has earned the highest regard of musicians and audiences around the world.

Barenboim conducted at Bayreuth for the first time in 1981 and is universally counted among the leading interpreters of Wagner since World War II. In 2003 in Berlin, he conducted all ten major Wagner operas over a two-week period.

In the early 1990s, a chance meeting with Edward W. Said, the eminent Palestinian-American and Columbia University professor of English and comparative literature, resulted in an extraordinarily productive dialogue, and friendship. Together, Barenboim and Said pursued the shared goal of peaceful coexistence in the Middle East and created the West-Eastern Divan Workshop, bringing together young musicians from Israel and the Arab world to make music together on neutral ground—originally at Weimar.

In 1999 Barenboim, against the wishes of the Israeli government, gave a recital for young Palestinian musicians in the West Bank and subsequently broke the unofficial ban on the public playing of Wagner in Israel.

The following is a brief excerpt from a series of public conversations between Barenboim and Said, published in 2002 as Parallels and Paradoxes. *Edward Said died the next year.*

EWS: What was the first Wagner you saw, do you remember?

DB: I think *Tristan*. So, I came to Wagner first of all from a purely musical and orchestral point of view. And I became fascinated with the way every element can really be examined individually, and with the whole idea of orchestration and of the weight and continuity of sound. And I became very interested in Wagner through his writings about music, and conducting, etc. So, this was the main thing that interested me first, and I did not occupy myself with the world of ideas at that stage.

This is what really fascinated me in his work, and in his writings about music. And his writing on the Beethoven symphonies and on conducting in general had a great influence on my whole way of looking at his music and of playing it. And then, as I became more and more connected with the pieces, I started preparing to conduct the operas, and this was the first time that I occupied myself with Wagner's writings on the subjects other than the music itself—i.e., the texts that Wagner wrote for his own operas and his ideological writings.

Question from audience: I was in Bayreuth in 1991, and I saw the production of *Das Rheingold* directed by Harry Kupfer, which had the most appalling anti-Semitism in it that I've ever encountered. . . . I couldn't understand how a Jewish conductor could take part in such a production.

DB: I can only tell you that if the violence of the action offended you, I'm sorry, and you have every right to have this kind of sentiment. The rest is your pure interpretation and imagination. I can assure you, I worked very carefully with Harry Kupfer on the production of this. We spoke openly on every subject that was treated in this staging. Never was there an intention, never was there an idea on Kupfer's side to make a Jewish character out of Alberich, or anybody else. There, I'm afraid I have to tell you this: it really says more about how you saw it rather than what it really was.

10

Charles Baudelaire

The most compelling of the French anti-realists, Charles Baudelaire (1821–1867), a supposed dandy and proponent of passive disengagement from bourgeois society, nevertheless was, like Wagner, on the barricades in 1848 and again in 1851. In 1857 he published perhaps the most influential poem of the century, Les fleurs du mal, *for which he was promptly convicted of both obscenity and blasphemy.*

Turning conventional values upside down, Baudelaire appalled established society by his decadent vision of unrepressed will and sensual pleasure, even satanism. Perceptive readers realized that he was exposing his own long journey downward into darkness, a journey as dreadful and courageous as Wagner's.

Like other French poets, Baudelaire was deeply influenced by Wagner's operas and essays. Early in 1860, Wagner gave three concerts in Paris, which Baudelaire attended.

Baudelaire immediately wrote Wagner, trying to explain how Wagner's music had "conquered" him. Like others under Wagner's spell, Baudelaire felt he had somehow heard this music before. He was struck mainly by the music's grandeur. It stimulated a sensual delight, a feeling as if rising in the air.

When Wagner read this appreciation, he recognized the presence of "an extraordinary spirit." He kept the letter. After the First World War, when German inflation was as its worst, Cosima Wagner gave it—no doubt as payment—to the Parisian couturier Jacques Doucet. In the meanwhile, with Charles Gounod, Gustave Doré, the Émile Olliviers, and a host of others, Baudelaire was to become a familiar figure at the composer's Wednesdays.

A year later, Wagner returned to Paris for performances of the revised Tannhäuser. *The ensuing "Jockey Club" scandal outraged Baudelaire. The following excerpt is taken from* Baudelaire, *by Joanna Richardson (1994).*

[After the 1861 *Tannhäuser* debacle,] Baudelaire, in Paris, lost himself in work. For three days, from 20 to 22 March [1861], from ten o'clock in the morning till ten o'clock at night, [Baudelaire] stayed at Pencoucke's, the printer's, going through "an enormous quantity of tobacco," and "improvising" his study of Wagner. The work was intellectually exhausting, but it gave him a sense of purpose. He was encouraged by a note from Wagner himself, inviting him to call. On 24 March, the third performance of *Tannhäuser* was given at the Opéra; and, harassed by the criticism which he found in Paris, Wagner withdrew his work. On 1 April, *La revue européenne* published Baudelaire's "Richard Wagner et *Tannhäuser* à Paris."

For Baudelaire, his appreciation of Wagner was more than a matter of national honor. He had recognized that Wagner's music revealed a new art, an art analogous to his own, an art which, despite its vagueness, suggested to different listeners the same general effects of light and colour and even the same visual images. Baudelaire had been haunted by the work of Poe and Delacroix. Now, once again, he had found a master whose work corresponded with his own instincts, emotions, and beliefs. Wagner had revealed a universal soul. The Overture to *Lohengrin*, and Wagner's "Lettre sur la musique," showed Baudelaire that he had done in poetry what Wagner was doing in music. He had done the same thing unconsciously in *Les fleurs du mal*. In an unfinished preface to the second edition of his poems, he had written that he had planned to show "how poetry touches music through a prosody whose roots plunge deeper into the human soul than any classicist theory indicates." It has been said that Baudelaire, alone in his time, was capable of instantly understanding Wagner's genius.

11

Michael Berger-Sandhofer

Michael Berger-Sandhofer is vice president of the Friends of the Salzburg Easter Festival and a longtime supporter of both the Summer and Easter Salzburg Festivals. Born in Salzburg in 1962, Berger-Sandhofer studied banking in Germany and law in Austria before receiving training in London and Chicago brokerage firms. In 1991 he returned to Salzburg, where until 2004 he was a private banker and asset manager for family-owned companies. Berger-Sandhofer has worked in a media company in London since 2005 and considers Salzburg his second home.

My Wagner Moment dates back to May 6, 1976, when part of Europe was rocked by an earthquake whose epicenter was in northern Italy. Registering 6.5 on the Richter scale, the strongest of three major tremors struck many European regions around 8:00 p.m. Greenwich Mean Time, which was 9:00 p.m. in my native Austria. The moment found me in Linz, the country's third largest city, and the one that gave its name to Mozart's famous "Linzer" Symphony. Just fourteen years old, I was there with my brother and mother to attend a concert version of *Die Walküre* at the well-known Brucknerhaus. We lived in Salzburg, but it was nothing to drive a hundred kilometers under the circumstances: Birgit Nilsson and Theo Adam were to sing the roles of Brünnhilde and Wotan in the beloved second opera of Wagner's *Ring* cycle.

A packed house eagerly awaited the beginning of Act II, when the famous duo would first make its appearance. Tension built throughout Act I until the instant when Siegmund was about to let fly his famous "Winterstürme wichen dem Wonnemond." Suddenly, the ceiling of the wooden concert hall crackled. The audience grew nervous; it seemed that *Winterstürme*—winter storms—were indeed about to disturb a lovely evening in May. When the crackling sounds gained force, the audience panicked and rushed toward all possible exits. The singers and much of the orchestra were quick to follow. In fact, no one really knew what was happening, especially since earthquakes were such a rarity in this part of Europe. But even though the performance was halted, my family and I remained glued to our seats, still under the spell of the engrossing first act.

Calm was restored a few minutes later. The performance resumed, and Act I was completed. During the intermission that followed, many people left, unsettled by the earthquake. The three of us had no intention of abandoning the hall, not least because the great Birgit Nilsson—my favorite singer—was about to make her entrance. As Act II began, I became even more excited to hear her voice resound through the trembling hall. And when she delivered her overwhelming "Hojotoho! Hojotoho!" I was utterly astonished. It was merely a concert version, and she was by then fifty-eight years old; nevertheless, her command of the stage, the sheer power and beauty of her voice, and her incredible, seemingly effortless top notes all worked in tandem to make that May 6 a Wagner Moment of seismic magnitude.

When Birgit Nilsson passed away on Christmas 2005 at age eighty-seven, I could only think of Wotan's words from the final scene of this opera that had so marked me: "Leb' wohl Du kühnes herrliches Kind!" (Farewell, you bold, wonderful child!).

12

Lord Berners

Gerald Tyrhitt-Wilson (1883–1950), the fourteenth Lord Berners, is widely, and warmly, regarded in England as the last of the British eccentrics. He was a considerable artist—composer, painter, poet, novelist, playwright—and also diplomat, humorist, and self-described dilettante. He wrote music for Diaghilev and the movies and was much admired by Stravinsky and Ernest Newman. His two autobiographies, First Childhood *and* A Distant Prospect *(from which the following passage is taken), go no further than his years at Eton. His political career was brief; he attended the House of Lords only once, because he said that a bishop stole his umbrella and he refused to go back.*

Sadly, he is better remembered today for his life at his country home, Faringdon, where he had his pigeons (harmlessly) dyed in pastels, as they still are, and built a great folly, a tower serving no purpose, to which he appended the warning: "Members of the Public committing suicide from this tower do so at their own risk."

It often happens that, when something new and unfamiliar crops up, one finds it immediately and constantly recurring, as if chance had taken the matter in hand and was bent on driving it home. The first thing that caught my eye when I went into Ingalton Drake's bookshop on the following morning was a little book called *A Synopsis of Wagner's Nibelungen* Ring. I can see it still—a slim white volume with red lettering. It was a matter-of-fact little work, written with no attempt at style or poetry, but its effect on me, when I began to read it, was like that of *Chapman's Homer* on Keats:

> Then felt I like some watcher of the skies
> When a new planet swims into his ken.

My interest in music had been aroused in the first instance by the sight of musical notation on paper. I was attracted to it pictorially. Wagner I approached along the paths of literature. As I read on, a wonderful new world unfolded itself. I passed enraptured through the green waters of the Rhine, into the resounding caverns of the Nibelung, up the pine-clad mountain slopes, across the rainbow bridge to the glittering turrets of Valhalla. I thought that the music must be wonderful indeed if it at all corresponded to this enchanted world.

I asked Delmer, who sniffed and said, "Oh, Wagner! I imagine it's just the sort of music you might like," from which I inferred that Wagner was one of those composers who "couldn't write a decent fugue." Wilson was equally unhelpful. "I haven't got any of his music," he said. "He only writes operas." Neither had the artistic Mrs. Elton anything to say on the subject, beyond that she had heard he was very highly thought of by certain people. Thus, for the moment, all that I had to go on was the fact, not devoid of encouraging implications, that my cousin Emily and the music master at Elmley didn't like Wagner, and that Deniston did.

A few days later, passing a music-shop in Windsor, I caught sight of a vocal score of the *Rhinegold* in the window. My heart gave a leap. So must Dante have felt when he saw Beatrice on the bridge in Florence, an incident portrayed in an engraving in Mrs. Elton's room. I burst into the shop with such violence, and demanded the score in so agitated a voice, that the shop woman looked for a moment as if she were about to call for help. Alas! It was twelve shillings—too much for my slender means. I was so crestfallen that the woman was moved to pity. Her expression softened.

"May I look at it?" I asked.

"Why, of course," she said, handing me the precious volume.

I turned over the pages feverishly. There they were, the Rhinemaidens swimming about in shimmering semi-quavers, Alberich clambering up from the depths of the Rhine to the accompaniment of syncopated quavers and rising arpeggios, the theft of the Gold, followed by a scurry of descending scales out of which emerged the majestic strains of the Valhalla motif.

The shop woman interrupted my trance by waving before my eyes a small paper-bound volume. "We have also the libretto," she said. "That is only a shilling." I bought it—it was better than nothing—and left the shop, casting a yearning backward glance at the score, which was being replaced in the window.

I walked on into Windsor Park and, choosing a secluded spot, sat down on the grass and began to read.

"The Rhinegold" by Richard Wagner
English Translation by H. and F. Corder

Prelude and First Scene

Greenish twilight, lighter above, darker below. The upper part of the scene is filled with moving water which restlessly streams from L. to R. Everywhere are steep points of rock jutting up from the depths and enclosing the whole stage; all the ground is broken up into a wild confusion of jagged pieces, so that there is no level place, while on all sides darkness indicates other deeper fissures.

I entered spellbound into the Wagnerian world. Windsor Park, the massive Castle, Eton, the whole world of reality became engulfed in the mysterious depths of the Rhine. My enthusiasm was not damped by the absurdities of H. and F. Corder's translation:

Alberich. Spoilt were your sport if 'stonished I stand here still. Near to me dive then, a poor Niblung longs dearly to dally with you.

Woglinde. He offers to join us.

Wellgunde. Is it his joke?

Alberich. Gladly I'd seek to encircle one of your waists, should you kindly descend.

Woglinde and Wellgunde. The languishing calf. Let us accost him.

It was all pure poetry to me. I read on until I was recalled once more to reality by the chimes of a distant clock warning me that I must hurry if I wished to be back in time for lock-up.

13

Günter Blobel

Günter Blobel is the winner of the 1999 Nobel Prize for Physiology or Medicine. He left East Germany in 1954, studied medicine in West Germany, and completed his studies at the University of Wisconsin in 1966, whereupon he joined the cell biology research group at Rockefeller University in New York. He won the Nobel for his work on the molecular analysis of cellular functions.

Blobel was in Dresden shortly before and shortly after the English and American firebombing of 1945. In 1994 he founded the Friends of Dresden to help rebuild the imperial Saxon capital, specifically the Frauenkirche—the largest Protestant cathedral in Europe—and a new synagogue. He donated the entire sum of his Nobel Prize money to this end. The restoration was recently completed. Wagnerians will remember that the Frauenkirche was the scene of the premiere of Das Liebesmahl der Apostel, *a massive choral work composed in 1843 by the Kapellmeister to the Royal Saxon Court, Richard Wagner.*

My most emotional Wagner Moments were in Bayreuth. Wagner's ghost floats over this city. Even though Wahnfried had been destroyed and only the exterior had been reconstructed, Wagner's spirit was still there. Particularly touching were the graves of Richard and Cosima under a magnificent tree, next to the little grave of their dog in the back of the garden. *Sic transit gloria mundi!*

14

Carol Ann Bogash

Carol Bogash has devoted her career to creating and managing opportunities for people of all ages and diverse backgrounds to better appreciate and delight in the arts, humanities, and sciences. She is a director of educational and cultural programs, a teacher, and a connector, bringing together individuals and organizations, nationally and internationally, to work together on projects, small and gargantuan, to promote a greater understanding about cultures, beliefs, and visions. She is a graduate of the University of Georgia and of Johns Hopkins University's Peabody Institute of Music. A passion for music, history, and science has figured consistently throughout her work in the Baltimore City Public Schools, the Baltimore Symphony Orchestra, Johns Hopkins University, the Smithsonian Institution, and the Washington Performing Arts Society.

My great-uncle was Joe Bogash, otherwise known in the music world as Giuseppe Boghetti. Uncle Joe, a tenor who studied at the conservatory in Milan and was a friend of Puccini, was the famed voice coach of Marian Anderson, Helen Traubel, Blanche Thebom, and Jan Peerce. He died before I was born, but his brother and my grandfather, Louis Bogash, remained lifelong friends with Peerce. Louis Bogash had a spectacular basso, and served as cantor in many synagogues throughout his very long life.

At the time I didn't recognize the short man with the very thick glasses as the great Jan Peerce. He was just my grandfather's friend and he sang really well. I remember Peerce's visits to my grandfather quite often as I was growing up; they would sing together around the kitchen table with a glass of schnapps. And, of course, they sang from *Die Walküre*—it was his singing Siegmund in that radio broadcast that brought Peerce to the attention of Arturo Toscanini. To a very little girl, just learning the piano, it was a moment in time that I remember quite clearly, with my grandmother hovering around the stove.

Throughout my career, both in the education and the symphony orchestra worlds, I have been touched by Wagner—most recently while serving as director of educational and cultural programs at the Smithsonian Associates for eleven and a half years. During that time I had wanted to present a major program on Wagner's *Ring* cycle—an in-depth look with noted speakers and good performers to help the general educated public to better understand the impact of this great music on our culture. It was with the help and guidance of the Wagner Society of Washington, D.C., and especially its chairman, Jim Holman, that we were able to create this fabulous weekend of programs, which attracted nearly 300 people. And, so it seemed a culmination of a lifetime fascination with Wagner that began with my grandfather and Jan Peerce.

Editor's note: See Wagner Moment 75: Jan Peerce.

15

Richard Bradshaw

Richard Bradshaw is the general director of the Canadian Opera Company. He has conducted more than sixty operas in his seventeen years with the COC and has established a reputation for adventurous programming and innovative productions. His cutting-edge collaborations with directors and designers from the worlds of film and theater—Robert Lepage, Michael Levine, François Girard, and Atom Egoyan— have garnered international critical acclaim and attracted new and young audiences. He has also increased the profile of the COC Orchestra with successful concerts and award-winning recordings.

For several years, Bradshaw has been closely associated with the building of the COC's new opera house, and in September 2006 he triumphantly conducted the first complete Ring *cycle in Canada at Toronto's new Four Seasons Center for the Performing Arts.*

Richard Bradshaw is a Senior Fellow of Massey College, Distinguished Visitor in Music and recipient of the degree of Doctor of Laws honoris causa, *University of Toronto; Honorary Fellow of the Royal Conservatory of Music; Chevalier in the Order of Arts and Letters of the Republic of France, and a Member of the Order of Ontario.*

"Reggie" (below) is Reginald Goodall, esteemed, not to say beloved, conductor at Covent Garden and, especially, Sadler's Wells (now called the English National Opera). Infernally modest, Goodall seemed forever content to remain in the shadows of the bigger names. Sadler's Wells took an enormous gamble in giving Goodall The Mastersingers of Nuremberg *in 1968, but it turned out a legendary success, securing Goodall's reputation. It also led the company to commit to its historic* Ring, *featuring not just Goodall but, in particular,*

Norman Bailey and Rita Hunter. I was privileged to see this Ring *on several occasions. When the Goodall recording was issued, we were astonished to learn that its running time is nearly seventeen hours, the longest of recorded* Ring *cycles and more than three hours longer than the Boulez. The ensemble was so committed, and Goodall so masterful, that nobody in the theater seemed to notice the glacial tempi. One of my great Wagner regrets is that I never saw the Goodall* Mastersingers.

It has to be Reggie conducting *The Mastersingers of Nuremberg* at the old Sadler's Wells in 1968, an evening which made you realize why everything in life can be all right really. It eclipsed even Rudolf Kempe conducting *Meistersinger* in 1962 at Covent Garden that I heard from the "gods" and thought was the most marvelous thing I had ever heard. Later, there was Reggie's *Ring* cycle, which influenced me greatly but now seems awfully slow on record, and the playing leaves much to be desired. It didn't seem to matter at the time. Reggie, more than anyone since Furtwängler, changed all our Wagnerian lives.

16

Frederick A. Buechner

Frederick A. Buechner has been a priest in the Episcopal Church for twenty-five years, since 1988 as Rector of All Saints Episcopal Church in Thomasville, Georgia. He is a past president of the no longer extant South Georgia Opera Company. He is married to a music teacher. His son is studying for a degree in musical education and his daughter in vocal performance.

I cannot help but note, in the context of Buechner's remarks, that Wagner's personal antipathy to the established church has never prevented believers from experiencing the most profound "Christian" spirituality and consolation in Wagner's music.

The Carnegie Hall concert to which Buechner refers was preceded by a concert in Berlin, performed five days after September 11, 2001—the first-ever joint concert by the Orchester der Deutsche Oper Berlin, the Berlin Philharmonic, and the Staatskapelle Berlin—in solidarity and friendship with the American people. In addition to the Tristan und Isolde *Prelude and "Liebestod," the concert included the Adagio from Mahler's Symphony No. 9 and the Allegro moderato and Andante con moto from Schubert's Symphony No. 8.*

Simply listening to the Tristan *Prelude on this recording, aware that it was offered to us as consolation by the German people in the aftermath of 9/11, is an almost unbearably wrenching Wagner Moment.*

My problem is that I have had three Wagner Moments!

The first came when I was four. My father had just bought a clunky old hi-fi about the size of a desk. One of the first records he played was the Prelude to Act III of *Lohengrin* (Leinsdorf). It was my "first time" hearing Wagner's music and I was hooked from that moment on classical music. Rock and roll and other pop always took a back seat to classical, because the *Lohengrin* Prelude taught me there was so much more substance to serious music. I wore that record out, which by the way still holds a place on my shelf.

Wagner Moment number two happened the year I graduated from college. The priest who nurtured my call and who was my spiritual and musical mentor (he died four years ago) was trying to get me into opera—with the singing. I told him that the only operatic vocal music I had ever heard was *La Bohème*. Although pleasant, it wasn't engaging enough for me to buy the records. Father Ralston went to his shelf and pulled out (would you believe it?) *Lohengrin* and put on the orchestral interlude in Act III where the armies gather on the banks of the river, with the chorus singing, "Heil König Heinrich, König Heinrich Heil!" That moment hooked me on opera, not just Wagner, but in time, Mozart, Verdi, and others.

Number three happened a month to the day after September 11, 2001 at Carnegie Hall. The Berlin Philharmonic was playing the Prelude and "Liebestod" to *Tristan und Isolde*. When the "Liebestod" began, with the strings doing that shimmering tremolo, I experienced the most wonderful balm, as if God were reaching His arms out from the stage to encircle, enfold, console, and comfort the audience.

I know this observation might make a lot of non-Wagnerian teeth fall out, but considering these three seminal moments, it's difficult for this priest not to think of the trinity (lowercase), and to label them respectively as father, son, and holy spirit: the first being a sort of bedrock, grounding moment for me musically; the second as directive, as in, "Listen up because you don't know what you're missing"; and the third as an abiding spiritual presence, not unlike that wonderful moment in Act II of *Die Meistersinger von Nürnberg* when the Night Watchman appears, with Walther and Eva hiding under the elderberry tree (Wagner Moment number four)—and you just know that, even though we have our individual and corporate trials with which to deal, in the end "All shall be well, and all shall be well, and all manner of thing shall be well."

17

Jeffrey Buller

Jeffrey Buller is a nationally recognized authority on classical literature and its influence on modern opera. He has written numerous articles on these subjects, as well as an acclaimed book about Wagner and his relationship to Greek drama, Classically Romantic. *Buller is an insightful, provocative, and entertaining lecturer and has been chosen in recent years by the Bayreuth Festival to give the English-language lectures during the festival. He is currently dean of the Honors College at Florida Atlantic University.*

Like all the other really important events of my life, my Wagner Moment arrived surprisingly late and in a way I could never have expected. It's not that I didn't listen to or care about Wagner while I was growing up. My parents had a fairly large collection of classical recordings—they were all those old, heavy 78-rpm recordings that took a stack at least an inch or more high to get through an entire opera—and they included all of Wagner's preludes. I vividly recall coming back from a music appreciation class in sixth or seventh grade and asking my mother where all of our Wagner recordings were. (On that occasion, I had probably heard "The Ride of the Valkyries" or some such thing that would've piqued the interest of a twelve-year-old boy and wanted to renew my excitement while the fever was hot.) But no, none of these were true Wagner Moments. When I went off to college some years later, I dutifully took a sizable collection of opera recordings (I had by then amassed my own collection on "modern" 33⅓-rpm vinyl), but the records I took were all Puccini, Verdi, and Cherubini; Wagner, alas, was nowhere in sight.

In fact, as late as when I was thirty-five, if you had told me that someday I would spend most of my vacations traveling about and talking to people about Wagner . . . that I would have actually written a book about *The Ring* (and not some obscure topic in Greek and Roman literature, the subject of my degree) . . . and that someone would repeatedly invite me to lecture on Wagner in Bayreuth of all places . . . well, I probably would've smiled politely, refilled your glass, and secretly thought how sad it was that you could no longer hold your liquor.

But then—as late and unexpectedly as it was—it finally came: My Wagner Moment. You see, I had recently moved from Iowa to Georgia to take my first full-time administrative position at Georgia Southern University, a school of about fifteen thousand students not far from Savannah. The library at Georgia Southern had its strengths in areas far different from those that were found at the college I had just left. Though that college had been but a fraction of the size of my new university, its classics holdings had been huge, and I had become used to finding almost without effort even the most obscure title on nearly any aspect of the ancient world. Yet Georgia Southern didn't even offer courses in my academic discipline; I was there to be an administrator, not to teach, and I was feeling the difference at once. I could easily order nearly anything I wanted through interlibrary loan, of course, but still I missed that serendipitous discovery of books that you encounter just by browsing the shelves. It was going to be harder than ever, I thought, to keep up the research I'd been doing on Sophocles. How in the world was I going to stay abreast of new ideas? Certainly, I could read the journals, but I couldn't expect the library to order everything on Greek tragedy just for me. I had no idea what I might be able to do to keep my scholarship active.

Yet, if the library holdings in classics were small, the stacks devoted to music were relatively well represented. The music program at Georgia Southern was both well respected and long established, so I decided rather abruptly to shift my research to a new area. Rather than writing about Greek tragedy itself, I'd start to write about all of those operas based on Greek tragedy. It would be a way of turning a long-standing

hobby and avocation into something a little more serious. And so, I wrote
a few works on baroque and classical operas that had classical themes, I
spoke at conferences about Offenbach's *Orpheus in the Underworld* and *La
belle Hélène*, and then, from some deep residue of early memory, I thought
it might be interesting to do a short piece on Wagner. After all, didn't
he have a classical education or something of that sort?

At about this same time, the Met was getting a lot of attention for its
"traditional staging" in the Günther Schneider-Siemssen *Ring* cycle, and
so I thought I'd see it as background for my research. What I didn't know
at the time was that the combination of that particular production and
my own intellectual life at that precise time was rapidly leading to my
own Wagner Moment. Only about halfway through *Das Rheingold*—I
recall that it was just as Wotan and Loge were descending to Nibelheim
and the anvils were sounding—I suddenly thought, "My God, that's it!"
And all at once everything in *Das Rheingold*, everything in the whole
cycle that I saw from that point forward—everything in Wagner's entire
oeuvre, for heaven's sake—abruptly seemed so . . . so . . . *classical*.

Don't get me wrong. I don't mean classical in the sense of Mozart
and Haydn, of course. And I don't even mean classical in the sense of
classical unities or classical restraint or any of the other connotations that
the word "classical" has received over the years. No, what I mean is that
I somehow felt—felt rather than knew—that what made Wagner work
for me was a classical sense of imagery. All at once, I felt attuned to the
way in which he related ideas to one another. The way in which he used
metaphors. The way in which he made the sound of his poetry somehow
reinforce an image in the music or onstage. Everything that I was experiencing was instantly far more classical than anything I had seen outside
of Aeschylus. In the darkness of the theater, I found myself thinking,
time after time, "Well, that means that this should happen next or that
such-and-such an image should appear or that the character over there
should say that." And every time I had this thought . . . it happened, just
as it was "supposed" to do. It was the closest I had ever come to feeling
that I was psychic. Except that it wasn't any extrasensory perception at
work—I was just suddenly becoming sensitive to the way a particular
artist's mind worked. I realized in a flash that more than a century apart,
Richard Wagner and I had somehow managed to read many of the same
books, and just like that, I felt that I "got" him.

Still flushed with the intensity of that moment, I wrote my first article on Wagner—a piece very dry and very academic—that related the images of pre-Socratic philosophy to the opening of *The Ring*. But while I was working on that article, I developed the idea for another essay, slightly less dry and maybe a bit less academic. And then another. And then another. And then finally a whole book of these articles.

Well, that's my Wagner Moment, perhaps filled with a little less grand passion than those of many of my esteemed colleagues. But Wagner's the sort of composer who can affect different people in different ways. He's at once the most intellectual of all romantic artists and the most romantic of all intellectual artists. And I have no way of knowing where he'll lead me next. I'm sure, however, that you already know. Perhaps you can tell me. And, if you do, I'll smile politely . . . and refill your glass . . . and . . .

18

Willa Cather

Willa Cather (1873–1947) remains among the most celebrated American novelists of the twentieth century, best known for her books about immigrants struggling to make a living in the Midwest in the 1800s.

The following excerpts are from "A Wagner Matinee," a deceptively disturbing short story about an aged and frail aunt who has left her dirt farm to visit her nephew in New York. He takes her, condescendingly and to fill the time, to an all-Wagner concert, only to watch in astonishment as she comes increasingly to life, into memory and passion and regret, and toward death.

The first number was the *Tannhäuser* Overture. When the horns drew out the first strain of the Pilgrim's Chorus, my Aunt Georgiana clutched my coat sleeve. Then it was I first realized that for her this broke a silence of thirty years; the inconceivable silence of the plains. With the battle between the two motives, with the frenzy of the Venusberg theme and its ripping of strings, there came to me an overwhelming sense of the waste and wear we are so powerless to combat; and I saw again the tall, naked house on the prairie, black and grim as a wooden fortress.

Soon after the tenor began the "Prize Song," I heard a quick drawn breath and turned to my aunt. Her eyes were closed, but the tears were glistening on her cheeks. . . . It never really died then—the soul that can suffer so excruciatingly and so interminably: it withers to the outward eye only.

From the trembling of her face I could well believe that before the last numbers she had been carried out where the myriad graves are, into the gray, nameless burying grounds of the sea; or into some world of death vaster yet, where, from the beginning of the world, hope has lain down with hope and dream with dream and, renouncing, slept.

The concert was over; the people filed out of the hall chattering and laughing, glad to relax and find the living level again, but my kinswoman made no effort to rise . . . the men of the orchestra went out one by one, leaving the stage to the chairs and music stands, empty as a winter cornfield.

I spoke to my aunt. She burst into tears and sobbed pleadingly. "I don't want to go, Clark. I don't want to go!"

I understood. For her, just outside the door of the concert hall, lay the black pond with the cattle-tracked bluffs; the tall unpainted house, with weather-curled boards; naked as a tower, the crook-backed ash seedlings where the dish-cloths hung to dry; the gaunt, moulting turkeys picking up refuse around the kitchen door.

19

Paul Cézanne

Paul Cézanne (1839–1906) is now firmly entrenched as the most admired—even venerated—and important artist of the nineteenth century, if not any century. Like Wagner's, Cézanne's accomplishments soared beyond any period or school. He is rightly seen both as a restorer of classicism and balance in painting, and as the prophet of modernism and deconstruction. More than anyone since Velásquez, he was considered by his peers, and virtually all great artists since, as "the painter's painter."

Cézanne painted during a period when Wagner and Wagnerism formed one of the most powerful movements in France. The following commentary on The Overture to Tannhäuser, *by Henri Loyrette, is taken from the Tate Gallery exhibition catalog,* Cézanne *(1996).*

Cézanne's depiction of an intimate, bourgeois musical is . . . not "Wagnerian" in any programmatic sense. . . . Even so, Cézanne's canvas is subtly responsive to the Wagnerian ethos. The painter had certainly discovered this composer in the early 1860s, when he was the subject of heated conversation in artistic circles in Paris. . . . Cézanne went so far as to "beg" [musician friend Heinrich] Morstatt to play some Wagner for him; in May 1868 he wrote him of his "happiness" on having heard "the overtures to *Tannhäuser, Lohengrin,* and *The Flying Dutchman.*" Cézanne doubtless knew Baudelaire's article "Richard Wagner et *Tannhäuser*

à Paris" [see Wagner Moment 10], written in the wake of the work's resounding failure at the Opéra and first published in *La revue européenne* in 1861 (also issued that year in pamphlet form). When, in the same letter from 1868, the artist implored Morstatt to visit him and cause "our acoustic nerves to vibrate to the noble accents of Richard Wagner," he was using language unmistakably reminiscent of the poet's evocation of the music's titillating aspect.

The Overture to Tannhäuser was conceived as a pictorial correspondence to the Wagnerian drama; in effect, Cézanne the *refusé* answered the "music of the future" so reviled in Paris with his own "painting of the future." But the canvas also subtly invokes the conflict at the core of the opera: "*Tannhäuser*," wrote Baudelaire, "represents a struggle between two principles that have chosen the human heart as their principal field of battle, namely flesh and spirit, hell and heaven, Satan and God. And this duality is established at the outset, and with incomparable skill, by the overture." Cézanne—himself engaged in perpetual struggle with these two "principles," as his work from the 1860s and 1870s makes clear—shows us one woman darning and another making music, one woman seemingly devoted to a domestic existence and another who dreams about the artistic life. Elizabeth and Venus—or alternatively, Martha and Mary, but with Cézanne we are left in the dark as to who has chosen the "good part"—each in her own world, so close yet so distant from one another, nurture their respective talents within the stuffy surroundings of a bourgeois interior. But for the time being, the "music of the future," laboriously approximated on a small upright piano, resonates in a void, stirring up only the flowers on the chintz slipcover and the arabesques on the wallpaper.

20

Marcia Davenport

Marcia Davenport (1903–1996) is best remembered for her novels East Side, West Side, The Valley of Decision—*both made into motion pictures—and* My Brother's Keeper. *She was also the daughter of the famous soprano Alma Gluck and spent much of her early life in opera houses around the world. In the 1930s she wrote a biography of Mozart and later was a commentator on the Metropolitan Opera radio broadcasts. In 1936 she published her first novel,* Of Lena Geyer, *from which the following excerpt—Lena's Wagner Moment—is taken. Wagnerians will remember that Richard Wagner's stepfather, and probable birth father, was named Ludwig Geyer.*

Lena went down one day to the opera house to a rehearsal, as she thought, of *Les Huguenots*, but found that she had made a mistake and that they were rehearsing *Die Walküre* instead. Heinrich Hermann, the German stage director, was in charge.

The rehearsal was going badly and Hermann was in a temper, wiping the sweat off his cropped head and running about with his shirt plastered to his shoulders. The troupe of Valkyries was particularly bad, so bad that Lena, more from malicious curiosity than anything else, stayed to listen to them getting scolded. Most of them . . . were Italian, and had no Wagnerian training at all. Then the Sieglinde had a cold and could not sing above a whisper, and the Brünnhilde had a voice like a foghorn. But the orchestra was not so bad and Lena found herself listening with awe to the stirring music. This was her introduction to a *Ring* opera . . . she had not dreamt of singing in any of them.

One of the Valkyries, however, now unwittingly opened up a whole new vista in Lena's life. The unfortunate girl faulted on the same passage three times in succession . . . and Hermann turned on her in a rage. "Get out of here, you washwoman!" he shouted in German. "Get off the stage and stay off!"

Then he saw Lena sitting in a corner.

"Who's that?" he roared.

One of the men told him she was a bit-player of Italian roles.

"What's your name?"

"Lena Geyer," she said.

"Italian?"

Lena got up and walked toward him. "*Nein*," she said, "*aber hier singe ich nur Italienischen rollen.*"

He took a good look at her and let out a rich string of Prussian oaths. "Take off your hat," he said, "and get over there with those girls."

"But *Herr Direktor*," Lena said, "I don't know *Die Walküre*. I've never studied it."

He scowled at her. "No? Well go home and learn this"—he ruffed through the pages—"and come back at nine tomorrow morning."

He turned back to the melee on the stage and Lena started home with his score under her arm.

21

Harry de Wildt

Harry de Wildt calls himself an Ameropean (actually Dutch American), in the mode of Henry James. He is a past board member of the San Francisco Opera as well as the Spoleto Festivals, in both Italy and Charleston, South Carolina. He thinks of himself as a world traveler and international socialite, but not a socialist.

The Great Awakening, as I call it, was when a friend played *Tristan* for me on his 33 rpm discs when I was around fourteen. With my youthful ardor I had come to love Mozart (yes, Mozart: he could do no wrong), Strauss (he could do little wrong), and Verdi. But all that changed after hearing Wagner. A new book opened in my life, which I have been unable to close, and now in my seventieth year the power of Wagner is stronger then ever.

Why? I have no idea! All I know is that when I play music at home, which I do for several hours a day, it is very difficult when I flip and roam through my very large collection of CDs to bypass anything by Wagner. I have to force myself to play something else, and as for "shuffle" play, forget it! When a Wagner piece randomly appears, I must stop what I am doing and listen to it. Certain pieces like Tristan and Isolde's duet, or *Götterdämmerung*, *Parsifal* (paralyzing *Parsifal*!), not to speak of *Meistersinger* or the first notes of *Rheingold*, will complete all my activities for the rest of the day. As for anything from the *Ring* cycle, that wonderful and ludicrous story about people who built a house they could not afford, most musical themes and motives are enough for me to make it impossible to continue doing what I am doing: I must listen. Harry, I say, be more careful next time. No more shuffle play for you!

I have always thought that if one, in this case me, was terribly ill with, let's say, incurable cancer and in pain, hopefully very old, it would be a breeze to swallow a bunch of pills, fly away on Brünnhilde's horse, jump into the fire with her, and, as they say, get it over with. What makes one stop is the thought of the people one loves and leaves behind. Obviously, Wagner does not cause the same reaction in many other people (just ask my wife Margot, for example), but many Wagnerites would agree with me, I think. And why is this so? Who knows? Perhaps Wagner's bigger talent, his meanness, ability to use and exploit people—who knows and who cares? Wagner has given me, and many people, more intellectual pleasure then anybody, and that should count for something.

22

Jonathan Dean

Jonathan Dean is education associate with the Seattle Opera. He has authored the surtitles for more than fifty productions at Seattle, including six Wagner operas, and his titles have been used at opera houses throughout the United States. He introduces opera to thousands of students each year, and The Theft of the Gold, *his adaptation for children of* Das Rheingold, *has been widely performed.*

Dean writes and lectures widely on opera and the humanities.

It was a Saturday morning in March, about 11:30 a.m.; the broadcast had started early owing to *Die Walküre*'s exceptional length. I was a weird thirteen-year-old, curious about things like myth, music, magic, and Wagner. And I was chiefly looking forward to the day because, after our eighth-grade school orchestra performed in the All-State Festival, we'd all be going bowling. I had had a crush on my stand partner for about five years; she had been warming to me all year in algebra class, and I figured if we played well at the afternoon's performance, I could make my move tonight.

But before the carpool left there was time to listen to the beginning of the opera. Peter Allen finished his spiel, and the first notes of the Prelude resounded through the house. The cold rain poured down in those shivering violins, the weary feet of the outlaw Siegmund thudded up and down the hills of the forest floor in the cellos, and I stood there, in the bright swath of sunlight shining through the high windows of the living room, by the big Kenwood speaker in the corner, wondering why it felt like I already knew this music. I had known about it for years. I knew the story perfectly well, and the Act III orchestral highlights; but that morning I really was listening to the music of *The Ring* for the first time. It was a sound markedly different from the sunny, warm, Mediterranean melodies of the many Italian operas I knew and loved. This was the sound of the North—a sound dark with the bitterness of beer (how could grown-ups drink that nasty stuff?), the sound of the cold, of clouds, of powerful muscles turning to lead with exhaustion, of strong arms rowing ships with dragons carved on the prow into fjords; the sound of the long, slow, steady defeat, and the indomitable spirit that fought the good fight regardless. The sound was new to me, and yet familiar; it was like a feeling I had known all my life but never named, an experience familiar from all those summers up in the great north woods, the feeling you get lying around a campfire on a beach in August, with the tall evergreens reaching up after the flying sparks toward all the stars of the northern summer. That feeling I recognized—here, now, was its sound. I heard only the beginning of the opera that day, baby steps in becoming a Wagnerite. But I understood, even in those first few bars: a love affair was beginning that would long outlast the infatuations of algebra class.

23

Achille-Claude Debussy

Debussy (1862–1918) is unchallenged today as a towering musical figure in the century after Wagner. He claimed in fact to be an anti-Wagnerian, freeing French music from the looming shadow of the Master of Bayreuth. But we know that Debussy's only opera, Pelléas et Mélisande, *is in many ways as "Wagnerian" as it is not.*

Debussy's is the most striking case—and perhaps the most successful—of the way all composers after Wagner had, in one way or another, to come to terms with the Wagnerian achievement.

The following passage, reflecting Debussy's experience in London at his first hearing of The Ring, *is taken from* Debussy: His Life and Mind, *by Edward Lockspeiser (1965).*

Debussy's artistic opinions, though dictated by an infallible instinct, were frequently mercurial. "Il aimait un jour la musique russe, un jour pas," notes Catherine Stevens. "Ceci faisait partie de son paradoxe." At times, also, they were almost unbelievably aggressive. Some kind of underlying apprehensiveness transformed into the most aggressive form of irony marks the article "Open-Air Music," in which Debussy proposes that "M. Gavioli, the famous maker of street organs . . . should be induced to make his instruments worthy of playing *The Ring*. Did not Wagner declare again and again that he could be understood only in France? . . . The Opéra does not shrink from playing *Pagliacci*; shrink then no longer from making street organs worthy to perform *The Ring*."

It is easy to see that Wagner almost invariably created this feeling of apprehension in Debussy's mind. He heard the complete *Ring* for the first time in April 1903 at Covent Garden and sent three articles on the work to [the newspaper] *Gil Blas* in the form of letters from London. The first dealt primarily with his impressions of London, which he was visiting on this occasion for the second time; the second was an assessment of the cast of *The Ring*, headed by Richter, and of the standards of production and performance at Covent Garden; and the third was a criticism of *The Ring* followed by a description of an evening spent at the Empire Music Hall in Leicester Square (the equivalent, he dutifully tells the readers of *Gil Blas*, "of our Folies Bergère").

Having no English, Debussy in London felt himself to be an anonymous personality, impressed, however, in the traditional manner of foreigners in London, by the courtesy of policemen, by a preoccupation with "respectability [he uses the English word] common to everyone from Joseph Chamberlain to the drunken news vendor," and also by the great number of idlers he noticed in the streets. An earlier visitor to London, Taine, had declared that there were no idlers in London. He was entirely wrong, said Debussy; English idlers are serious-minded, he notes, and seem to have a goal in view. They do not idle, like the French *flâneurs*, for the mere pleasure of idling. He wrote his first dispatch in a building on the Embankment. He had so far only heard *Rheingold*, and was anxious lest these London letters became "too personal."

The main article, entitled "Impressions of *The Ring* in London," does not conceal the extent to which a musical mind can be ravaged by Wagner.

> It is difficult to imagine the effect made even on the toughest mind by the four evenings of *The Ring*. A quadrille of *Leitmotive* is danced in the mind in which the theme of Siegfried's horn forms a curious partnership with that of Wotan's Sword, while the "Curse" theme persists in performing a *cavalier seul*. One is more than obsessed; one is subjugated. You are no longer yourself, you are merely a *Leitmotiv* walking or wandering about in the Nibelung entourage. Normal civilized behaviour cannot henceforth prevent us from greeting our fellow creatures with cries of the Valkyries: "*Hojotoho? Heiaha! Hoioho! Hoioho!*" Even the London news vendor will be shrieking, "Heiaho, my lord!" How tiresome these helmeted figures clad in the skins of wild animals become by the end of the fourth evening!

And Debussy proceeds to sling his well-known gibe at Wagner's conception of the *Leitmotiv*: "It suggests a harmless lunatic who, on presenting his visiting card, would declaim his name in song." Debussy was understandably censorious of Wagnerian mythology and of the Wagnerian plots. But of the music he wrote in terms of the highest praise. "Suddenly, effects loom up of unforgettable beauty. They are as irresistible as the sea. . . . One does not criticize a work of such magnitude as *The Ring*. Its too sumptuous greatness renders futile the legitimate desire to grasp its proportions."

And he grandiloquently concludes: "'Wagner can never quite die. He will eventually feel the cruel hand with which time destroys the most beautiful things. . . . Some splendid ruins will, however, remain, in whose shade our grandchildren will dream of the past greatness of a man who, had he been but a little more human, would have been great for all time." In the same year, replying to a questionnaire organized by the *Mercure de France* on the German influence in France, Debussy prophetically declared: "Wagner, if one may express oneself with some of the grandiloquence that belongs to him, was a beautiful sunset that was mistaken for a dawn." Those are words in which Debussy was speaking from the heart. They show that, over the period from Wagner's death to the outbreak of the First World War, the seed of pessimism in Wagner's work had taken root far beyond Germany.

Toward the end of his article the train [taking Debussy back to Paris] passes through the Normandy countryside. The apple trees are in blossom and the overwhelming Covent Garden *Ring* is left to recede into the widening shades of Debussy's London memories.

24

John Louis DiGaetani

John DiGaetani is a professor of English at Hofstra University and an acknowledged authority on the nineteenth-century English novel and stage drama. He is a highly regarded critic of contemporary English and American plays and playwrights and is the author of A Search for a Postmodern Theater.

DiGaetani is, in addition, a prolific and influential writer on music. His books include Carlo Gozzi: A Life in the 18th Century Venetian Theater, an Afterlife in Opera; Puccini the Thinker; Opera and the Golden West; Richard Wagner and the Modern British Novel; *and* Wagner and Suicide. *He is also the editor of* Penetrating Wagner's *Ring (1978) and the recently published* Inside The Ring *(2006).*

I remember very well my first and most influential Wagner Moment. I was in graduate school and on my first trip to Europe during the summer of 1966. Back then the flights cost a fortune, but once you were in Europe everything was very cheap, thanks to the strength of the American dollar. I landed in Paris and, despite my jet lag (my favorite disease, I must admit), rushed to the Paris Opéra and was horrified to discover that all that was being performed for the whole week was *Tannhäuser*. Back then I liked opera but did not like Wagner, yet I was so eager to see that beautiful opera house that I bought a cheap ticket for *Tannhäuser* for the next night.

I remember the performance as too long but sometimes electrifying. I particularly remember Rita Gorr as a sensual Venus. But the most exciting moment for me came at the beginning of the second act when Régine Crespin entered as Elisabeth and sang "Dich, teure Halle." I remember how stirring the music was and how convincing her performance of that role and especially that monologue was. I did not know what she was singing, but I found the music of that moment so thrilling that I decided I had to learn more about Wagner. I completely forget who sang *Tannhäuser*, alas. Coming from an Italian background, I had been warned about the dangers of Wagnerismo, but I was definitely electrified by Crespin's Elisabeth.

My next stop on this first European trip was Rome, and at the Terme di Caracalla there was a performance of *Lohengrino*—in Italian. There too I enjoyed much of the performance and was fascinated to discover that this was where the "Wedding Chorus" was from, but found myself agreeing with Rossini, who said of Wagnerian opera that it had "wonderful moments but terrible half hours." I liked some of the opera's moments but felt that the operas obviously needed to be cut since they were simply too long and boring and contained too much *recitativo*.

But as I listened to the music on recordings and followed the libretto to understand the text, I found those dull passages actually became quite fascinating. As I listened more and came to understand more, I eventually concluded that the trouble with Wagner's operas is that they tend to be too short.

25

Plácido Domingo

Very little needs to be said here to introduce Plácido Domingo. To have reached near immortality as a dramatic tenor, that most revered and treacherous of professions, speaks for itself. One might also note his continuing accomplishments as conductor, Zarzuelan, and advocate for opera; his general directorships at Washington and Los Angeles; his development of, and kindnesses to, young singers; and the inexhaustible expansion of his repertory.

For our purposes, it is necessary to make some rather obvious points: first, that Plácido has become, over the last thirty years, the world's best Wagner tenor, and second, that this was something he never had to do; his reputation was made long before he turned to Walther and Lohengrin. The Wagner Moment he has provided is an extraordinary insight both into the power of Wagner's art and into Plácido's sensitivity and commitment to his own as well.

It is an established fact that in opera as in the legitimate theater, the person portraying grief should not shed a tear, because in doing so the emotion becomes choked rather than projected to the audience. Experienced actors will have shed that tear in rehearsal and thus, when it comes to the actual performance, can be completely convincing to the audience by simply recalling how they felt the anguish in rehearsal.

Among the more than one hundred different roles I've sung, there have been some that call for tears. Only on very rare occasions did the raw emotion get the better of my performing technique and I succumbed to the raw emotion of shedding that actual tear.

However, there is one role, namely Siegmund in *Die Walküre*, that occupies a very special place in my performing experience. Every time I lie dying in Act II, tears well up in me that I cannot suppress, because I realize that my death was caused at the instigation of my own father, the god Wotan. The reason for this overpowering emotion is the combined genius of Wagner as a librettist and composer. I would call this my personal Wagner Moment.

26

Les Dreyer

This letter appeared in The New York Times *on May 1, 2005, in response to a commentary on Wagner by the critic Anthony Tommasini. The Tommasini article to which it refers can be read in its entirety (see Wagner Moment 94).*

Letter to the Editor

Wagner may have been a raging megalomaniac and a ranting anti-Semite, as well as the composer whom Hitler deemed dearest to the Aryan soul. Yet when I, a Jew, joined the Metropolitan Opera orchestra in 1961, I was mystified to find that several of my Jewish colleagues—elderly Holocaust survivors from major German opera houses and orchestras—actually relished playing Wagner. I recall one violinist proudly showing us novices his Vienna Opera fingerings for murderous passages in *Götterdämmerung*, which he knew from memory. I questioned him about his emotions when playing Wagner. With moist eyes, he bitterly complained about the numerous *frevelhaft* (sacrilegious) cuts in the Met score.

27

Leslie Dunton-Downer

Leslie Dunton-Downer has written extensively for the American composer Augusta Read Thomas. Their first collaboration, the chamber opera Ligeia, *was commissioned by Mstislav Rostropovich, who conducted the world premiere in Évian in 1994. Awarded the International Orpheus Prize under the jury president, Luciano Berio,* Ligeia *has received productions in Europe and America. Dunton-Downer was also librettist to the British-born composer Bernard Rands for* Belladonna, *which premiered in Aspen in 1999 under the baton of David Zinman. With the* New York Times *European cultural correspondent Alan Riding, she is coauthor of* The Essential Shakespeare Handbook *(2004) and* Opera *(2006).*

My early takes on Wagner had everything to do with being an American born in 1961. First came television's Silly Wagner, especially in Chuck Jones's brilliant Warner Brothers cartoon *What's Opera, Doc?* By the time I was attending R-rated movies, the Vietnam era had ushered in Crazed Military Wagner. For years following the release of Francis Ford Coppola's *Apocalypse Now*, Wagner could evoke only Robert Duvall's face and helicopters.

As a student, I liked to go dancing with friends at the Pyramid Club in New York City's East Village. There, in 1984, we lost our minds for disco remixes of Malcolm McLaren's "Madam Butterfly," a recording that offered instant certification from a major counterculture guru to set out and explore classical opera. Soon, my roommate joined those who had sprung for recordings of the Puccini. And meanwhile, a few rock musicians in our circle searched for irresistible opera tracks in used record stores. They occasionally found the odd aria or overture that all of us were persuaded to find "wicked cool," the highest possible assessment. At this point, I ran into Anti-Italian Wagner.

Somehow, social pressure enforced an unwritten law: if you were madly in love with Puccini or Verdi, then you must scorn Wagner. When I came across images of Wagnerian Heldentenors and divas in sepia-toned Teutonic gear and garb, I dutifully saw them as ludicrous or contemptible. At times, they made me feel embarrassed for the vocalists posing in them. At others, I was rather embarrassed for myself to live on the planet that spawned them. At their worst, the old photographs made Wagner seem boring. This was my Embarrassing and Boring Wagner phase. But at least these incarnations were less troubling than Politically Scary Wagner. The composer's anti-Semitism, the service of his operas to German nationalism, and the subsequent Nazi monumentalizing of him and his work—all conspired to make "Wagner" automatic shorthand for "No thanks."

My Wagner Moment came at a point when I was emotionally raw, questioning everything, and deeply unsatisfied by assumptions, especially those toted around for decades. In 1992, as a novice opera librettist, I was catapulted into a world of professional musicians. Some offered standard moanings about the horrors of the "Wagnerian vibrato," or the catastrophic Wagnerian engulfment of words by music, or the unbearably humorless quality of Wagner's imagination. But even strident complainers insisted that, when it came to marrying dramatic action with music today, "Everything goes back to Wagner." So, there was no getting around it. I was going to have to struggle against decades of amassed clichés and received wisdom and *actually listen* to Wagner.

I began with *The Ring*. The cycle's dreaded duration and the sheer enormity of its structure made it the perfect candidate to check off the list first. From there, I figured, the going would be less rough. Looking over *The Ring*'s squadron of operas in general preparation for the ordeal, "The Ride of the Valkyries," from the second in the sequence, *Die Walküre*, caught my attention. Of all operatic passages, surely this one was the most freighted. For many, it had become virtually synonymous with Wagner, or even synonymous with opera itself. For me, it instantly conjured up a jumbled montage of Elmer Fudd and Bugs Bunny, balls of napalm flame, frumpy braided wigs, horned helmets, and Hitler. My intention was to listen to *The Ring* from start to finish, an opera at a time. But I couldn't resist a quick dip into the Segment of Segments, thinking that it would steel me for the colossal chore that lay ahead. The recording was of the 1989 production conducted by Wolfgang Sawallisch in Munich. I found the track.

What I heard produced the kind of rip-your-head-off-at-the-neck-and-shake-it-up-and-down seizure more suited to a Metallica concert than to an adult's living room. Over and over, I listened to "The Ride of the Valkyries" in that Please Knock Me Out Just One More Time phase of music-lover infatuation. Then I called unsuspecting friends, played it to them over the phone, and begged them to indulge me in long conversations about each detail. Some were requested to listen to the passage more than once, grilled for new reactions, and then urged to bond with me emotionally over the thrill of hearing something so familiar as if for the first time. When it was too late to place calls in any time zones where I knew potentially dormant Wagner fanatics, I replayed the passage on my own, listening to specific aspects of the music and trying to hear them independently. After that, I took in the selection with headsets, without them, at higher volume, with boosted treble, while following the libretto, while disregarding it, and any other way I could think of to get to the bottom of its bewitching secrets. "The Ride" was different each time, and remains mysterious to my ear no matter how much I listen to it, read about it, or hear from its interpreters how it works and why it is so extraordinary. The next day, the opening bars of *The Ring*, from *Das Rheingold*, proved just as enthralling. But by then I had already been bitten.

28

T. S. Eliot

Thomas Stearns Eliot (1888–1965) was born in St. Louis when his parents were forty-four years old. He prepped there and in Massachusetts and by 1910 had both bachelor's and master's degrees from Harvard. He spent the next academic year in Paris, where he was tutored in the French language by Henri-Alban Fournier, who, under the pseudonym Henri Alain-Fournier, published, in 1913, the influential novel Le Grand Meaulnes.

He returned to Harvard in 1911 to pursue a Ph.D. in philosophy, where he studied, as Wagner had, Buddhist and Indic philosophies. When World War I broke out, Eliot cut short a visit to Germany to take up a scholarship at Oxford. In 1915 he worked as a teacher and bank clerk, married, and published The Love Song of J. Alfred Prufrock. *Eliot's masterpiece,* The Waste Land, *was published in 1922. He took British citizenship in 1927.*

Eliot's background with respect to Wagner, and Wagner Moments, remains something of an enigma. On the one hand, he "never found it necessary to discuss Wagner at any length" (William Blissett, Wagner and The Waste Land*). "There is one highly important, yet maddeningly brief, item of corroborative evidence. When Igor Stravinsky and Eliot finally met, near the end of Eliot's life, 'we managed to talk to talk that afternoon, nevertheless,' Stravinsky writes, 'and although I hardly recall the topics, I remember that Wagner was one; Eliot's nostalgia was apparent and I think that* Tristan *must have been one of the most passionate experiences of his life.'"*

The following passage is taken from Father Owen Lee's Wagner: The Terrible Man and His Truthful Art *(1999).*

The poem that, to my generation in college, best spoke for our century was T. S. Eliot's *The Waste Land*. I remember that there were well-thumbed copies of it strewn about Trinity College back in the forties. At St. Michael's College, in the days of Marshall McLuhan, we students eagerly organized our own seminars to discuss it outside of class. Even the engineers on this campus knew it and cited it. It was our poem, even if we didn't understand every grim prophecy made in its maze of quotations.

The Waste Land, emblematic of so much in our century, contains two direct quotations from *Tristan und Isolde*, two quotations from *The Ring*, and, as Professor William Blissett of this university has pointed out, many subtle echoes of *Parsifal* as well: even the familiar opening, "April is the cruelest month" (cruel because it holds the promise of rebirth), can be related, via Eliot's reference to the Starnbergersee where Wagner's patron Ludwig II was drowned, to the Good Friday scene in *Parsifal*.

That Eliot quotes strikingly from Wagner in perhaps the most famous poem of our century does not of itself speak of a pervasive Wagnerian influence. Eliot quotes from any number of other figures: *The Waste Land* is a depiction of Western civilization in decay, reduced to butt-ends, to fragments of Sappho, St. Augustine, and Shakespeare shored up against the winds of twentieth-century change. The West is going under. Only the Eastern thunder of the Upanishads speaks peace. Soon it will all be over. We're closing up the pub. Eliot telegraphs that headline throughout the poem in unpunctuated capital letters: HURRY UP PLEASE ITS TIME.

But of all the figures of Western civilization, from Petronius to Jessie Weston, quoted in the poem, Wagner is the most central to its themes. He too saw Western civilization as headed for disaster: he ended his four-part drama about the Nibelungs with a world-destruction myth that was not part of his sources. And, as Eliot perceived, Wagner thought that Eastern wisdom could save the West. He patterned, not just the end of *The Ring*, but much of *Tristan* and *Parsifal* on Buddhist teachings.

But that is not the end of Wagner's influence on *The Waste Land*. The music of Wagner's operas, especially from *The Ring* onwards, is largely composed from leitmotifs or, as Wagner called them, G*edachtnismotive*, "motifs of memory"—recurrent fragments of music ranging from two notes to not much more than twelve, associated at first with personages or objects or actions but by the end of the fifteen-hour cycle charged with additional meanings through their repeated interaction with one another. That is what is going on in *The Waste Land* as in no poetry since the patterned, shifting, interacting images in the choral odes of Aeschylus. Wagner knew Aeschylus. He read him constantly while composing *The Ring*, and he fashioned a new kind of musical composition after the Greek's poetic techniques. Eliot in turn knew Wagner, and fashioned a new kind of poetic composition after the German's musical techniques. It was that haunting, allusive, essentially Wagnerian use of quotations in *The Waste Land* that caught the imagination of my student generation at this university, and indeed of the civilized world.

29

Kenneth R. Feinberg

Ken Feinberg was appointed by the Attorney General of the United States to serve as the special master of the federal September 11th Victim Compensation Fund of 2001. In this capacity, he developed and promulgated the regulations governing the administration of the fund and administered all aspects of the program, including evaluating applications, determining appropriate compensation, and disseminating awards. He recently published a book entitled What Is Life Worth? The Unprecedented Effort to Compensate the Victims of 9/11. *In 2006 Feinberg became president of the Washington National Opera.*

My memorable Wagner Moment occurred when I was a teenager in Brockton, Massachusetts, and managed to secure a copy of the first complete *Ring* cycle of Georg Solti on the old Decca phonograph record label from the Brockton Public Library. I had heard excerpts of *The Ring*, but the complete Solti set provided me a unique opportunity to immerse myself in the entire *Ring* story and music and had a profound impact on my love of Wagner and determination to learn more. I quickly signed out of the local library all of Wagner's operas and began an intense review of his entire recorded inventory. Today, I probably own about 1,000 Wagner recordings of complete operas, excerpts, and orchestral interludes. I have also made two different trips to Bayreuth to witness firsthand *The Ring* and managed to have dinner with Wagner's grandson a few years ago.

During my tenure as administrator of the September 11th Victim Compensation Fund, with all of its pressure and intensity, I managed to secure some relief by listening to Wagner operas and attending as many concerts and live performances as I could. It helped immeasurably.

Martin Feinstein

In 2006 Washington—and the music world at large—lost a giant. In his long and distinguished career, with Sol Hurok, running the Kennedy Center for the Performing Arts, and the Washington Opera, Martin Feinstein transformed the cultural life of the nation's capital. He was also my friend, and I include here a tribute that I wrote for the Wagner Society of Washington, D.C.:

No matter where they are in the world, anybody concerned with the performance of great works of art mourns the death of Martin Feinstein. Members of the Wagner Society of Washington, D.C., are among those people, and hope that we can be forgiven if we feel a special affinity to Martin and his uncountable achievements.

He was the first recipient of our Society's Award, and among our first lecturers, sharing his unrepressed enthusiasm for the "Winterstürme." He once told me that his deepest regret at the Washington Opera was not to have had the opportunity to stage a Ring cycle, and surely the WNO's current Ring will be dedicated to his memory. None of us will forget Maestro Domingo's leading the "Siegfried Idyll" at the Kennedy Center memorial tribute to Martin.

Most of all, we will miss Martin as a friend, and hope that we can, in his honor and in his shadow, continue to make a small contribution to our city's regard for great music.

Having lived fourscore years and loved opera from the first note I heard at age twelve, there have been hundreds, if not thousands of Wagner Moments in my lifetime. It was all the more thrilling, then, to hear Plácido Domingo's Siegmund the last time at the Met in 2004.

I am amazed and thrilled by the strength of his voice, his ability to project the humanity of the characters he portrays, conveying the full range of human emotion. All this could be summed up by saying: "Plácido just gets better and better."

31

Aurelius Fernandez

Aurelius Fernandez had a long and distinguished career with the United States Foreign Service, after which he helped found, in 1996, the Wagner Society of Washington, D.C. He remains its president today. In 1999 Aury was a proud spear carrier in the Washington National Opera's production of Tristan und Isolde.

It was not until the summer of 2000 that I saw the Bayreuth Festspielhaus for the first time and experienced two Wagner Moments that overshadowed all the others in the preceding half century of my life. The Moments concern the site and the sound of that incomparable 1876 wooden structure on the Green Hill, the shrine for Wagner pilgrims. On the outside, the structure has been the subject of more negative than positive aesthetic architectural critiques; but most agree that, on the inside, it is the best place in the world to listen to Wagner's music.

The site. On seeing the Green Hill for the first time, I was overwhelmed and knew that I was in good company. Like Birgit Nilsson, "I still remember the exact moment when I first saw the Festspielhaus . . . I thought my heart must burst." As soon as I arrived in Bayreuth, I hastened in jet-lagged drowsiness to see the Green Hill. A music teacher from Michigan and his son were there for the first time, too. We breathlessly took photos of each other posed in front of the floral arrangement with the Festspielhaus in the background. As we took the photos, I recalled the comment of Frederic Spotts, who says in his magisterial classic on the history of the Festival that "Wagner would find it [today] almost as it was when he last saw it in 1882." It was the launching pad for the famous *Bayreuther Geist*—the Spirit—that Wagner let loose to influence music around the world. It was also the site where Cosima launched her famous "Bayreuth bark"—the *Bayreuther Konsonanten-Spuckerei*, as Ernest Newman phrased it. After so many years of looking and longing over photos of the Festspielhaus, it looked much larger than I expected; but all that gentle architectural homeliness was beautifully in place!

The sound. When the lights went out before the curtain, the only things I could see in the near total darkness were several small red emergency-exit signs. I heard a scattered cough or two here and there, but they seem to end as the "Bayreuth hush" set in—that silence of anticipation of a truly sublime musical experience. As with others in the audience, I waited silently in the armless chairs that some (though not I) find uncomfortable. Soon, the music from the invisible orchestra permeated the auditorium. As I sat in the darkness, it was difficult to say exactly where the music was coming from; it seemed, awesomely, to be coming from all over. The mystery of the haunting musical sound is partially explained by the unique reverberation time in the wood and canvas structure. As the sagacious and witty Rudolf Sabor phrased it: "The listener experiences the aural sensations of a musical fly trapped inside a double bass!"

32

Sherman Finger

Sherm Finger is an accomplished musician and one of the country's finest golf professionals. After an outstanding junior golf career, Finger achieved All-American honors three times at the University of Southern California, followed by a successful career on the Professional Golf Association Tour.

Finger has been one of the country's outstanding teaching professionals and has been a leading golf professional in the Chicago area for more than thirty years. He is a past president of the Illinois Section of the PGA and has received numerous honors and awards.

Sherm and his wife, Marty, are deeply involved with the Lake Forest Symphony, the Ars Viva Symphony Orchestra, and the Chicago Master Singers.

The music of Richard Wagner changed the direction of musical composition. Wagner demonstrated that sonata form, symphonies, the differentiated songs that made up an opera or oratorio, and the theme-variation-recapitulation critical to the fabric of classical music were no longer a necessity. Wagner introduced a new chromaticism, changing keys as successive notes went up or down the scale.

Melody no longer needed to be confined in aria, but could be expressed as a stream of consciousness. Continuous music filled entire acts of his operas, and many of those acts lasted more than an hour.

Wagner introduced musical ideas only a few notes long and later repeated these same few notes to keep this idea in the minds of his listeners.

My first Wagner Moment was listening to the Overture to *Die Meistersinger von Nürnberg.* The wonderful, upbeat music creates excitement in the audience. The rising chromatic notes and chords are unique and make one eager to hear what is to come. The melodic beauty of *Die Meistersinger* is extraordinary.

The first act of *Die Walküre* is the epitome of Wagner's stream-of-consciousness style. Leitmotif after motif pervades this music. Great depths of love, fear, and hope are expressed as never before. Wagner is able to arouse feelings of a depth seldom evoked in music. He led the way to evocative musical expression, which we hear in the Impressionists, the discordant twentieth and twenty-first century composers, and the movie scores of today. A good Wagner performance is always a deeply emotional experience.

33

Benjamin Foster

When Ben Foster and I studied Arabic together, at university and also in Lebanon in the 1960s, I knew he was a superior student to me, but I had no idea how much better: Ben is the Laffan Professor of Assyriology and Babylonian Literature at Yale and curator of the Yale Babylonian Collection. He is the country's leading expert on Mesopotamian and especially Akkadian literature, as well as the social and economic history of Mesopotamia. Among his many books, articles, monographs, and translations on these subjects is his highly regarded translation of The Epic of Gilgamesh *(2001). Foster is also an accomplished musician.*

Even lovers of viols and harpsichords are given Wagner Moments. Open-air performances of the Philadelphia Orchestra were prime summer-evening recreation during my grade-school years. Stokowski even prevailed on the Pennsylvania Railroad to mute its bustling freight yards, opposite the park, while he conducted for a rather rowdier set, including well-nourished mosquitoes, than the one that frequented the Academy of Music. One June evening, perhaps around 1950, shimmers in my memory. The trombonists and their fellow brass players, seeming extra radiant and splendid in their white coats, bore us aloft on their march with the Meistersingers. Somehow you were sure that they too felt the extra magic in a piece they could probably play from memory. Then did the genius of Wagner, and no other, rule us all.

34

Peter Gelb

On August 1, 2006, Peter Gelb became general manager of the Metropolitan Opera, with responsibility for both the administrative and creative aspects of the world's largest opera company—the most recent challenge in an extraordinary career in music.

Gelb's Met career began as an usher, when he was in high school and his father was managing editor of The New York Times. *Like Martin Feinstein (see Wagner Moment 30), his training in artistic management came under Sol Hurok. He has produced twenty-five opera telecasts, including the 1990 Met* Ring, *broadcast on PBS over four consecutive nights and later released on DVD. He also produced, among many others, Emmy Award–winning films of Rostropovich and Horowitz, whom he managed late in the pianist's career.*

Before coming to the Met, Gelb was head of Sony Classical Records for ten years, a period of innovation, growth—and controversy, during which he added crossover music, film scores, and the commissioning of new music to the classical repertoire.

In the summer of 1987 I was making a documentary about Herbert von Karajan—the only film ever made about the iconoclastic conductor while he was alive that he didn't direct himself. The film was shot over a six-week period during the Salzburg Festival, which Karajan ruled imperiously. There was an unwritten law that Salzburg did not produce Wagner operas, leaving that musical turf to nearby Bayreuth, but that didn't stop Karajan from scheduling Wagner in some of the Salzburg concert programs anyway.

At the time, Jessye Norman was approaching the pinnacle of her career and had been invited to sing with Karajan for the first time. Together they had chosen the "Liebestod" from *Tristan*, even though there was some debate within musical circles as to whether it was too high for Norman's voice. It was late in Karajan's career, and his powerful grip over his musical empires of Berlin and Salzburg had already begun to decline—along with his health and some of his mental acuity. Earlier in his career he had been a master strategist when dealing with orchestras and soloists, adroitly bending them to his artistic will while avoiding confrontations. Recently, however, he had been clashing publicly with his orchestra, the Berlin Philharmonic.

His next target was Ms. Norman. Anticipating her arrival, Karajan began questioning the singer's vocal range, complaining that she was more mezzo than soprano (even though the maestro had extended the invitation to sing the piece in the first place). By the time she arrived, he had worked himself up into something of a stew. He bypassed the usual initial piano rehearsal and instead summoned her to the Festspielhaus stage, where he met her for the very first time in front of the full Vienna Philharmonic. He commanded her to sit near the podium and then proceeded to rehearse the orchestra for several hours, never allowing her to sing a single note. "I wanted her to hear how it should sound," he told me afterward.

Luckily, Ms. Norman kept her cool. As she left the stage after the rehearsal, I not so innocently asked her (with cameras running) what had happened. "I didn't sing a note," she said and giggled.

Norman was of course allowed to sing in subsequent rehearsals, and the performance was a triumph. Karajan, though, was not entirely convinced. "It was good," he told me moments after the performance. "But she's still a mezzo."

35

Raymond Geuss

Raymond Geuss earned his doctorate in philosophy in 1971 at Columbia and Freiburg. He taught at Heidelberg, Princeton, Chicago and other universities before emigrating to Britain in 1991. He now teaches in the Faculty of Philosophy at Cambridge. His most recent book is Outside Ethics *(2005).*

Melody as Death

Human memory is a tricky phenomenon. We remember so easily what we take pleasure in recalling, and also what we most definitely do not wish to recall. Sometimes if one is quick and nimble enough, one can even catch the process of "reconstructing" one's past in memory in the hope, that is, that one can recall the original impression and also the gradual way in which it began to fade, shift, and be transformed. Very occasionally, the original experience is so vivid one cannot help thinking it is preserved in the mind in a form that excludes serious error or uncertainty about it. I have had two dozen or so moments like that in my life, and one of them was connected to Wagner.

My father was a steelworker in the Fairless Works of U.S. Steel in Fairless Hills, Pennsylvania. Access to music in a working-class household during the early 1950s was limited. There was the local (AM) radio, my grandmother had a primitive gramophone, and some people had

45-rpm record players that spouted a few moments of pop or rock music; that was about it. My father had a pleasant but completely untrained light tenor voice, and he sang in the U.S. Steelworkers' Chorus, a group of a dozen or so men who put on dark blazers—provided by U.S. Steel in an attempt to gain public good will—six or eight times a year and sang Christmas carols, Broadway show tunes, and perhaps the odd light classical piece.

When I was about eleven or twelve, I had a school friend from a slightly more affluent background than mine who invited me over one afternoon and played an LP record on the new hi-fi system his parents had just purchased. The recording was of the beginning of Act III of *Die Walküre*, "The Ride of the Valkyries." I distinctly recall two impressions I had in quick succession that are among the most vivid I have ever received. The first was simply that of being overwhelmed by the richness and complexity of the sound, and the electricity of those crisply executed initial upward-reaching flourishes (in B minor, as I now have learned to call it) in the first four bars. More indescribable flourishes in the horns and bassoons followed, and then the alternation of the ascending motif with descending slurred quintuplets in the violins.

The second impression I recall is my disappointment, in fact complete and utter dejection, when the horns and the bass trumpet entered forte at bar 13 and an easily discernible motif emerged very clearly as an individual theme from the general whirl of sound. I remember thinking: "Oh, no. There is a tune in this after all." Obviously what I had especially liked about the beginning was that there was no discernible melody, and it disturbed me that the entrance of the horns and bass trumpet retrospectively turned what I had previously heard as a mere pattern of dotted-eighth notes (starting in the horns and bassoons in bar 5) into the precursor of a "tune." What did I have against tunes? I knew only music with clear "tunes"; what I had liked about this music was that it seemed to be articulated sound without a distinct melodic line. This was something utterly outside my previous experience. To hear for the first time music that was structured but not standardly individuated was exalting; it was a liberation, for which I have never ceased to be grateful.

The experience of liberation, genuine as it was, was not the whole story, though. There was also the sense of being let down when there did turn out to be a melody after all. I would not have been able to express it clearly at the time, but I believe that my reaction to this initial encounter with Wagner had its power partly because it reactivated a memory of another event in the then recent past involving music and my father that had called forth in me intense but deeply ambiguous feelings. Wagner himself was well aware, as I discovered much later when I read his theoretical works, that the well-defined thought, sentence, image, or musical theme is not as good a vehicle for ambiguities as a wash or ocean of sound is.

My father suffered from Crohn's disease—a severe, and in his case recurrent, ulceration of the small intestine for which, at the time of its onset in 1948, there was no treatment except surgery. So in a series of operations he gradually had most of his small intestine removed. During my childhood I was always told to be ready for him to die at any moment—this is what the doctors were said to be predicting—and the loss of most of his intestine seriously impaired his ability to absorb nutrients, so no matter how much he ate, he looked like a skeleton. In between bouts of the disease and recovery from surgery, however, he continued to work in the mill and to sing in the Steelworkers' Chorus.

One Christmas they gave a concert, the high point of which was the carol "O Holy Night." The end of this had an *ossia* section, with the top variant ending on a long-sustained high note, I believe a high C with *fermata*. Most of the men could not sing the upper variant at all; my father could just barely, although he had a tendency to run out of breath and cut off the fermata slightly before the director wanted. I watched and listened at the rehearsals as my father tried again and again to sustain the note to full value, and again and again failed. The evening of the performance was tense. At the crucial point, I could hear my father's voice soar out, alone, in the upper *ossia*, loud and clear above the dull sound of the rest of the chorus, like the sharply defined theme in "The Ride of the Valkyries." He hit the final note, held it firmly for its full value—this seemed to go on forever—and collapsed on stage. Individuation, of course, is tantamount to death, in that only that which steps out of the amorphous state of undifferentiated mere existence, and takes on a distinct shape of its own, comes to live at all—and perhaps sing its own *ossia*—but then must die. My father was not dead, but had, it turned out, merely hyperventilated.

Wagner's Valkyries were predatory scavengers, picking up corpses from the battlefield, slinging them over their saddles, and making off with them. When I listened for the first time to my friend's LP of the beginning of Act III of *Die Walküre* in 1958, the appearance of an individuated "tune" meant, I assumed, that "they" were coming for "him"; he would have to be warned (or not). It was, however, as I well knew, already too late. My father already looked like a walking corpse, and, sadly, the Valkyries had long since got him. This was a terrifying but also oddly attractive and deeply depressing train of thought. Wagner, as we all know, prided himself on having access to hidden depths in the human soul, areas that human society—what he called "the State"—had declared taboo: the inextricable mixture of love for, fear of, hatred of, pride in, and disappointment with one's father is one of these. How could fifteen bars of mere orchestral music open that abyss? I have no idea, but I know it happened. One could not, perhaps, ever close it, but one could try to turn away. The price for doing that would be an impoverishment of one's life, and this is a price that I have done my best not to pay. Wagner's music has remained an integral part of my life ever since.

Thomas Grey

Thomas Grey is associate professor of musicology at Stanford University. His fields of specialization include Wagner, nineteenth-century opera, the history of musical aesthetics and criticism, romantic music, and visual culture. He is the author of Wagner's Musical Prose: Texts and Contexts, *and editor and coauthor of* Richard Wagner: The Flying Dutchman. *He has written innumerable articles and reviews in leading musical journals and compendia. From 1999 to 2001 he was editor-in-chief of the* Journal of the American Musicological Society.

Instrumentalizing Wagner

December 1974. I was sixteen and anticipating, with a nigh insatiable hunger, the C. F. Peters piano-vocal score (arranged by Felix Mottl) of *Götterdämmerung* for Christmas. I had become aware of Wagner only about a year and a half before that. I recall playing from a red-bound collection of Classical warhorses, arranged for piano, the Prelude to Act III of *Lohengrin* back in the summer of 1973, intrigued by its great gusto and a sense that I already knew this music, somehow, without knowing it, exactly.

At the end of summer, returning home to Connecticut, I acquired an RCA recording of Toscanini conducting some of the Wagner basics, including the first- and third-act *Lohengrin* Preludes. (What I did already "know" of Wagner at that point came from having perused some years earlier a chapter in an old arts appreciation volume, c. 1947, full of ominous insinuations about Wagner's baleful influence on Nazi

Germany, which seemed mainly to consist in having provided a hoard of Teutonic cliché; I don't think Jews were mentioned.) In the meantime I had begun to seek out Wagner in bits and pieces: excerpt discs of Karl Böhm's Bayreuth *Tristan* (Nilsson and Windgassen) and Karajan's *Rheingold*, as well as Bruno Walter's Act I of *Die Walküre* (Melchior and Lehmann).

I was fascinated by the words and music alike but paid rather little attention to the singers, beyond noting their generally odd appearance from the cover photos. (I had also brought back from a summer trip to Germany a cheap disc of excerpts from *Lohengrin*, with a very tacky picture of some blonde woman, not the actual soprano, in sky-blue chintz or gauze.) I also learned most of the standard excerpts from a collection of piano arrangements, some of Liszt's and a handful by later arrangers. Here I was generally satisfied with the titles or incipits provided, even though I really was interested as to what this music was "about." "Am stillen Herd in Winterszeit" or "Morgenlich leuchtend im rosigen Schein" were sufficient cues to imagining the tenor of the rest. (The former I recall finding very apt as I played it by candlelight in the course of a three-day power outage in late November 1974, the very same Connecticut ice storm, it must be, that provides the backdrop to Ang Lee's film.) The "Liebestod" often ran through my mind, but mainly in its Lisztian version, not Nilsson's. During a brief stint of running cross-country I would urge myself on with it, continually recycling its upwelling sequences to the point of exhaustion, calling vaguely to mind images of breathing and collapse from the text.

Thus it was that I greedily anticipated the delight of a whole Wagner score to consume, and *Götterdämmerung* no less. When Christmas finally arrived I was delighted to discover not only the previewed piano vocal score, but also a complete LP recording of the opera. It was from the budget Westminster series issued in the early 1970s, conducted by Wolfgang Sawallisch with competent but hardly outstanding singers. I had earlier glimpsed the *Walküre* from this set in Gallup & Alfred's music store on Asylum Avenue in Hartford and had been amused by the cheesy, cheeky 1960s era wit of its cover art (a naked, long-haired model, torso only, covering hear breasts with two Volkswagen hubcaps), although I wasn't entirely comfortable with such an attitude toward my newly discovered cultural icon.

The humor of the *Götterdämmerung* cover was more strained, or at any rate oblique: two hands, probably of the same model, reaching down and crumbling a large cookie (well, I suppose I saw the point). Of course I absorbed this recording scrupulously and with great pleasure over the following months, though I could not now say without looking them up who the singers were. But the score remained the key treasure. In addition to silently singing through stretches of it at the piano, I decided to achieve a fuller immersion by playing the entire Prologue and Act I into a feeble Wollensack reel-to-reel tape recorder we happened to have about the house, so that upon playback I could perform the vocal lines on an alto recorder (the instrumental kind, that is) I had only very imperfectly mastered around that time. Wagner's musicodramatic policy of avoiding ensemble singing made this at least theoretically possible. In the end, however, I'm pretty sure I gave up on this approach not far into the first act.

So, at that key moment in the middle of the 1970s, *Götterdämmerung* was the ne plus ultra, a sublime and necessarily isolated operatic peak (and not necessarily the weaker for my programmatic ignorance of *Siegfried*). Excerpts from *Götterdämmerung* were pressed into service in observing important emotional events: Siegfried's funeral music upon the early death of a very devoted beagle–basset hound mix (not without some compunction at this mingling of aesthetic experience and "real" feeling), and above all the final, apocalyptic, and redemptive pages of the cycle to mark fundamental passages, like the eve of moving away for good from Connecticut and my hometown, the site of a still awkwardly unrealized early love, at the beginning of the next summer.

Only the recording could do justice to these high purposes, admittedly, not hacking out the score at the piano, let alone piping out Brünnhilde's lines on an ill-tuned recorder, struggling hopelessly with the accidentals and high notes. With time, naturally, I came to accept and appreciate Wagnerian singing, as I came to accept and appreciate other things, as they became possible, or necessary. Yet I still see as somehow fundamental this early practice of "instrumentalizing" Wagner, by which I mean not just wresting the music from the voices, but applying the music, and the whole "conception" (however exactly I saw that), to life, and learning or imagining what role music could play in it.

37

Stuart Hamilton

Stuart Hamilton has for many years been one of Canada's great vocal coaches. He has worked at one time or another with such eminent Wagnerians as Jon Vickers, Maureen Forrester, Ben Heppner, and Adrienne Pieczonka, and such non-Wagnerians as José Carreras, Isabel Bayrakdarian, and Richard Margison. He has also over the past fifteen years appeared as a regular guest on the Metropolitan Opera Quiz.

As a kid in a small city on the Canadian prairies during the Great Depression, I hardly knew what the word opera meant. There was the ubiquitous Gilbert and Sullivan society which, when feeling racy, branched out with, perhaps, *The Chocolate Soldier.*

The wife of one of my schoolteachers told me that she had been to Chicago to see *Lohengrin* (she pronounced it "Long-gerr-een"). She said that it was about a knight in shining armor, and that it was "just lovely."

Not long after, I was twiddling the dial on our old radio when out of the loudspeaker came three incendiary voices, singing their heads off. I had stumbled on the Metropolitan Opera broadcast and caught the last five minutes of *Faust.* I loved it. (I still do.) The announcer said at the end that they would be back next week performing Wagner's *Tannhäuser.* I had no idea that this was the same man who had composed the lovely "Long-gerr-een." The following Saturday, Milton Cross described the action of the first scene. (It sounded rather dirty.) When the horns played the first notes of the overture, the hairs on my head stood straight up and didn't come down for the next four and a half hours. (Well, maybe they came down in the intermissions, I don't remember.) Toward the end, as the great melody thundered out with the chorus, I was awash with tears. My father, a good man who couldn't carry a tune, came into the room and exclaimed, "For God's sake, what's the matter with you now?"

I didn't know how to tell him that I had just discovered my life's vocation.

38

Pamela Jones Harbour

From 2003 to 2006 Pamela Jones Harbour was the commissioner of the United States Federal Trade Commission. She received degrees in both music and law from Indiana University.

At the tender age of fifteen, my singing voice was "discovered" by my father, who had prayed all his life for the gift of song, and who believed his prayers were answered through his youngest child and only daughter. Soon thereafter I began taking lessons with a local vocal instructor, and in the spring of my seventeenth year I set off for an audition at Indiana University's School of Music. I was admitted as a performance major and began my classical music education in the fall of 1978, joining a host of other talented classmates—one of them being the young violin prodigy Joshua Bell. I soon discovered that many of my classmates were steeped in music theory, composition, and history, as compared to my more modest and relatively recent introduction to music.

My Wagner Moment came (and remained) during the infamous Indiana University Music History 101 "drop the needle" examination, where the professor literally dropped the needle (before the days of CD players, of course) at the beginning, middle, or end of a musical composition and the student had to identify the composer, composition, and movement. I could always recognize when the needle was dropped on any of Wagner's pieces. I nodded with satisfaction when I recognized *Tristan and Isolde* and giggled with glee when I identified the "Valkyries" theme in Wagner's *Ring*, envisioning the earth goddess Erda's eight immortal and warlike daughters. Wagner was the first composer to use music as a means of influencing, enhancing, intoxicating, and conquering. And when I hear Wagner, I continue to be inspired, moved, elated, and vanquished to this day.

39

Daniel Herwitz

Daniel Herwitz is director and Mary Fair Croushore Professor of Humanities at the University of Michigan, teaching also in the philosophy and art history departments, the School of Art and Design, and the program in film and video. He was previously chairman of the philosophy department at the University of Natal in South Africa and has published a book of essays on that country's transition to democracy, Race and Reconciliation.

Having earned a Ph.D. at the University of Chicago, Herwitz has taught and written in the fields of contemporary philosophy, aesthetics, art, architecture, music, film, and "global culture," including the culture of universities.

With a father like Daniel's, it is hardly surprising that Daniel has risen so high and gone so far. Many (but perhaps not all) Wagnerians will applaud this breaking of the applause barrier after Act I of Parsifal.

It was Easter, sometime back around 1982, and the Metropolitan Opera was doing a special performance of *Parsifal.* I'd been to a number of Wagner productions there, but never had Lincoln Center seem so filled with German-speaking people. It was as if a call had gone out over the radio gathering the tribes. I'd been to the Met many times but seldom heard so little English spoken, so little of the patois of New York. My father arrived a short time after me, dressed in his usual patois of distressed items—Birkenstock sandals, burgundy Indian vest, white shirt with Nehru collar, Patek Phillipe watch.

I had the sense he was the Indian chief out of a book by Karl May to these people; there were plenty of stares. He was a fashion designer, a Jewish immigrant off the docks with a family that had quickly, in one generation, risen from factory and tenement to rich and rewarded, and whose mantle of America was one in which you had to dance to your own drummer whole cloth, like he was beating out "The Ride of the Valkyries." Naturally my father adored the swan-songing seductiveness of it all—of Wagner I mean—while being less than adoring of its European temple. His temple was one in which the rabbi chanted the refrain in a language even Siegmund would not have understood.

"That one I wouldn't go to" is the punch line of the old joke about why a man alone on a deserted island spent his time building two temples, one at each end. My father went to both, believing the point was to have it all, but with the gluttonous irony of a man about to blow up the works. This did not seem to sit well with the Easter occasion, but what the hell, he figured: anything can happen in New York.

At the end of the first act, after time is stilled in the contemplation of an endlessly repeated major-third ostinato, the wound is revealed (without Vicodin or Prozac to heal the suffering), the ritual is abided, and the audience is instructed (by the composer) to sit in awestruck and overwhelmed silence. Thus is the Christian service—which is not silent—transformed in the halls of art and the audience given its lessons in how to behave.

Scanning this audience, at this moment, as it stilled itself in preparation for entry into the third ring of the first ring of Valhalla, my father became, for a moment, wholly intoxicated with himself. He rose from his seat, swayed like a warrior about to spring into action, raised his hands toward the stage, and screamed out—*screamed out*—at the top of his lungs, "Attaboy, Wagner! What the fuck, unbelievable, fantastic buddy, over the top!"

The audience was too well behaved to pummel him, even though that may have been written into the score. But what crossed my mind, in addition to the mortification of the weak-willed, the well-behaved, the loyal-to-the-end, was another time, ten years before, when the Chicago

Symphony, conducted by Mitch Miller, had been playing the Overture to *Tannhäuser* in Grant Park on the Fourth of July.

Fourth of July, ninety degrees out, and the park filled with 100,000 people, and when the music ended a young man, obviously high on cocaine (or was it Wagner alone?), leaped onto the stage, into the shell, and called out at the top of his lungs, "That was fucking unbelievable! That Wagner is amazing, totally wonderful, my mind is fucking blown!!" Seconds later at least twenty Chicago cops emerged from backstage, from under the pit, even from strategically placed palm trees, and buried him. The young man was African-American; otherwise, I think the police would not have dived at him whole hog. So there he was, taken away in cuffs, still awestruck and overwhelmed, just like Wagner had asked for.

The moral: you can't predict who will catch the Wagner bug, nor what will happen when you do.

40

Adams Holman

Adams Holman is an accomplished pianist and a musicologist specializing in nineteenth- and twentieth-century music. He has worked at Carnegie Hall since 2002.

When I was young, I never had much use for opera, much less for Wagner, even though I grew up in a household in which opera (especially Wagner) was highly valued. Later, as a music major in college, I immersed myself in the piano and symphonic literatures while essentially ignoring opera. (I remember listening to the first act of *Tristan* for a music history class assignment and reacting with complete indifference.) Nevertheless, thanks to my parents I had plenty of exposure to Wagner growing up, including a memorable performance of *Die Meistersinger* at the Lyric Opera of Chicago and, later, a complete *Ring* cycle (Götz Friedrich's production for Deutsche Oper Berlin) at the Kennedy Center.

My attitude changed dramatically at the Metropolitan Opera House in spring 1991 during the Grail scene in Act I of *Parsifal*. To say I responded to this scene in a visceral and intensely emotional way would be an understatement. In addition to the beauty of the music and the intensity of the action onstage, however, I was also deeply moved by the interaction between Parsifal and Amfortas. Like Parsifal, who, upon catching sight of Amfortas crying out in pain as his wound starts to bleed afresh, reflexively clutches his own heart, I had the sense that a profoundly significant event in my own life was unfolding in front of me. (Also like Parsifal, I didn't yet realize why.) As if to underscore this, late in the scene, when Parsifal was offered bread and wine by a knight of the Grail, he refused both, spreading his hands and shaking his head in wordless confusion.

When the act was over, I felt too overwhelmed even to begin to sort through my emotions, so I left the opera house and walked across Lincoln Center Plaza to the fountain, where I simply stood for several minutes, staring at nothing. Suddenly a familiar voice greeted me from behind, and my father clapped me on the shoulder. (He had just returned from Europe and, knowing I was planning to attend this performance, had taken a taxi from the airport and bought a ticket at the last minute.) "Wasn't that something?" he asked me. "I was crying my eyes out!" I nodded. We chatted for a few moments; then he climbed into a taxi and was gone.

In the years since, I've come to realize that in a way, I "met" my father for the first time that night, not so much because of our shared experience—i.e., our reaction to the Grail scene, which we did not discuss—but because it seemed to me that for the first time I could remember, he and I were occupying common emotional ground. Again like Parsifal, who never knew his own father but who comes to see Amfortas as the father he never had (though he does not understand this in Act I), I found myself engaged emotionally with my father on a clearly defined level, even if I was still consciously disengaged on others. That is, although I followed *my* path to Wagner (as opposed to one that had been suggested to me or laid out before me), I arrived at much the same place as he had. "So this is what Wagner means to him," I thought as I returned to my seat for Act II. "Now I understand why."

41

Marilyn Horne

In 1981 Opera News *said that Marilyn Horne is "probably the greatest singer in the world," and not many disagreed. During a career ranging from 1954 to 1999, she was "without a doubt one of the greatest mezzo-sopranos in opera history and is probably the greatest Rossini interpreter ever."*

My own Rossini Moment came at the Met in the 1970s, during a dazzling Horne performance of L'Italiana in Algeri.

For several years I had sung the Immolation Scene from *Götterdämmerung* with orchestra in concert. Usually I found that the conductors liked to program it with "Siegfried's Rhine Journey" and "Siegfried's Funeral March." Normally I made my entrance after the funeral march, but at one concert—and I am sorry I cannot remember who was conducting—I was asked if I would sit through the first two pieces and then stand to sing, allowing the conductor to go straight into the Immolation Scene without a break. It was then that I was lifted out of my seat during the "Funeral March." From then on I only did it that way, and made the decision that I still hold true: that "Funeral March" is the most powerful music ever written. I was sitting in the midst of it and each time I was overwhelmed. A unique experience.

My own sole Wagner appearance onstage was as Gerhilde in *Die Walküre* in 1959 in Naples, Italy, with an imported company of many Americans. It was a lot of fun, and because I was about a foot shorter than all the other Valkyries, they loved putting them all in long blond wigs and me in a long black one. In addition, the chain mail came down to my knees. The blondes were put in platform shoes and I was in flats. I was thereafter known backstage as "La Valkyrietta."

Added note: The very first opera I ever saw was the San Francisco Opera production of *Tristan and Isolde* with Kirsten Flagstad and Ramon Vinay, conducted by William Steinberg at the Shrine Auditorium in Los Angeles. I certainly do remember it. I remain a Wagner freak.

42

Hans Hotter

From the recent translation of Hotter's (1909–2003) Memoirs: *"Hans Hotter was one of opera's most influential and profoundly moving artists of the twentieth century. His imposing fame and austere, high-browed profile made him an ideal figure of tragic dignity, unequalled in his era as Wotan, Amfortas, the Dutchman, Scarpia, and the Grand Inquisitor in* Don Carlo, *and several Strauss roles, including three world premieres of that composer's works."*

I have often told people that one doesn't become a genuine Wagnerian until, at a performance of Die Walküre, *one can't wait for Wotan's second-act narration. This quip usually gets the intended laugh, but there is much more than a kernel of truth in it. It was my privilege not just to listen to Thomas Stewart sing this passage, but to listen to him talk about it, especially in the context of the entire approach to singing Wagner. Stewart became the world's great Wotan (and Sachs) in the era after Hotter, who did much to help Stewart when he started singing at Bayreuth.*

The following passage, also taken from Hans Hotter: Memoirs *(2006), translated and edited by Donald Arthur, describes Hotter's approach to the narration, as coached in his initial portrayal of Wotan by Clemens Krauss, one of Strauss's librettists and an eminent Wagner conductor.*

It was my great good fortune that the first Wotan took place in Munich and that my boss, Clemens Krauss, was present at the birth of this portrayal as both midwife and godparent. How many suggestions he gave me! Suggestions that would more than surprise some of today's singers!

For example, Krauss would say, "Don't forget that it was never Wagner's intention to have *The Ring* performed outside of Bayreuth, and the acoustics in the Festival Theater are outstanding, not least because of the covered orchestra pit." Today's conductors don't take into consideration that the dynamic markings (*piano, forte,* and so on) were intended only for the Festival Theater and its unique acoustics. In other words: the composer would have altered those markings, modifying them for performances outside Bayreuth. Then Krauss told me, just as Römer had, that Wagner always instructed his singers to interpret his roles, especially the dramatic ones, strictly in *bel canto* style.

How fortunate I was to be instructed and advised by such mentors! How many *piano* passages, for example, in *Die Walküre,* are simply overlooked by so many musical and stage directors, when they should be insisting on the singers interpreting them that way.

While I was preparing for rehearsals in Munich, Krauss imparted to me an especially important insight: "Don't make the mistake of listening to the people who claim that Wotan's narration in the second act is so unbearably long. On the contrary: base your interpretation on the view that this narration, as measured by the many things that happen in it, is actually too short. You must keep thinking to yourself: how am I going to accommodate so much text, how will I make the many significant words understandable to the audience, with so little music? Ergo: the narration isn't too long, it's too short." At first I found it hard to understand such a new approach, but then I gradually began to gain an understanding of what I was being told. I am convinced that I owe it to advice like that, when after the experience of more than a hundred performances, people credit me with successfully structuring a diversified interpretation of that dauntingly difficult scene.

43

Christine Hunter

Chris Hunter is among the most generous and effective patrons of opera in America. As head of the executive committee of the Washington National Opera since the mid-1980s, she provided invaluable guidance to that company and its historic growth. She is currently chairperson of the Metropolitan Opera. Hunter is likely to be seen in opera houses around the world—including Bayreuth.

One of my first opportunities to attend a performance of Wagner lives on today as one of the greatest opera performances of my lifetime. In 1971 I was fortunate to hear *Tristan and Isolde* at the Metropolitan Opera. Birgit Nilsson and Jess Thomas were the two principals scheduled to sing that evening. The house lights dimmed, but instead of the orchestra's first ominous phrase, the curtain parted and a gentleman in coat and tie walked forward. The audience audibly groaned, anticipating the loss of one of their beloved stars. Mr. Thomas was indeed indisposed, but it was announced that Jon Vickers had agreed to take his place. A huge roar of approval surged through the auditorium, and I immediately realized that something special was about to occur.

It was a new production by Gunther Schneider-Siemssen, with August Everding directing. A marvelous supporting cast surrounded the principals, and Erich Leinsdorf conducted. By the time Nilsson and Vickers began their extraordinary love duet, they were in top form. The stage became completely black except for a spotlight focused on the two lovers. Slowly, almost imperceptibly, they began to rise, as did the intensity of the music.

I was so completely transfixed that after a period of time, I began to think that I too was rising. At one point, this feeling was so unnerving that I looked to my right to see if I really had begun to float. Of course, I was still in my chair, but for several minutes my whole being had been lifted to another place. When I took my eyes off the stage, I also realized that I was not the only person in this emotional state. The person sitting in the box next to me, who happened to be Richard Stillwell, had tears streaming down his face. So did everyone in the box—so did I! What a sublime Wagner Moment!

44

Linda and Michael Hutcheon

Linda Hutcheon holds the rank of University professor in the Department of English and the Centre for Comparative Literature at the University of Toronto. She is author or editor of more than fourteen books on contemporary postmodern culture. She is also the associate editor of the University of Toronto Quarterly. *In 2005 she won the Canada Council's Killam Prize for the Humanities for scholarly achievement.*

Michael Hutcheon is professor of Medicine at the University of Toronto, where he is the deputy physician in chief for education for the University Health Network. His extensive scientific research publications encompass a number of areas, including pulmonary physiology, bone marrow transplantation, and AIDS. He has also published in the fields of medical education and the semiotics of both cigarette and pharmaceutical advertising.

Their collaborative, interdisciplinary work on the cultural construction of sexuality, gender, and disease in opera has been published in a book entitled Opera: Desire, Disease, Death *(1996). Their second book, a study of both the real and the represented operatic body entitled* Bodily Charm: Living Opera, *was published in 2000. Their latest book,* Opera: The Art of Dying, *was published recently by Harvard University Press and is a study of how operas help us deal with our mortality.*

This is a story of passion: his, and (later) hers, for Wagner's music dramas. He had been quite smitten from the start with an early Canadian Opera Company production of *Die Walküre*, though somewhat thwarted in his affection by the subsequent *Siegfried*, which convinced him he knew nothing about *The Ring* (and he did not blame his youth and medical school, which took up most of his time). She, the stubborn student of literature, resisted the Wagnerian charms; she thought Wagner really needed a good editor. Both *Die Walküre* and *Siegfried* were for her just too long, too wordy. *Lohengrin* and *Tristan und Isolde* confirmed him in his infatuation, and her in her resistance.

Then the Canadian Broadcasting Company presented the 1988 Harry Kupfer production of the Bayreuth *Ring* on radio. She had just finished a book on postmodernism—that strangely self-conscious, parodic, yet historically grounded moment in western culture that became a topic of both popular and academic debate in the 1980s (and after). So she was likely primed to respond as she did—not to *The Ring* or even initially *The Ring* directed by Kupfer, but to the audience response to it. She was not used to hearing directors and designers booed with such vigor; she was fascinated as the host of the show, Howard Dyck, tried to explain to listeners the cause of the audience's discontent. The more the host tried, the more she realized she had to see this production: self-reflexive, parodic, yet historically resonant, Kupfer's vision of Wagner's *Ring* was postmodern. Or so she rapidly convinced herself.

By the time he returned home from work that day, she was planning their trip to Bayreuth. He was thrilled, of course, but concerned. She in turn was to be put off by neither his discouraging words about the difficulty of obtaining tickets nor his reminder that she didn't even like Wagner. This was postmodern; she had to see it. Persistence and luck paid off: tickets were miraculously obtained. Being academics, they prepared for the Bayreuth experience as academics would: they took a course. They spent hours each week with the *Ring* scores and recordings.

They all but memorized the texts. She got increasingly hooked, despite herself: Wagner will do that to you. She had been warned.

August came. Prepped and eager, they sat in the dark theater awaiting those first E-flat major chords, little knowing that they were about to have the most powerful dramatic experience of their lives. It was

Wagner's doing, for sure; it was also Harry Kupfer's. This *Ring* was amazingly exciting theater—postmodern theater, of course.

Feeling postmodernly vindicated—and now seriously addicted—she succumbed to the lure that has snared so many others. They returned twice more to see this production, and going into the last act of *Götterdämmerung* for the final run of the final year, they were still excited and held in the grip of the drama, not knowing what Kupfer and his fine-singing actors would do next. The directorial changes from year to year were proof of the presence of a thinking director who cared about music and words and, most important, drama. When the disgruntled traditionalists rose to boo Kupfer this time, five years after her first puzzled experience of this sound, there was a very strong contingent of cheering (postmodern) spectators, including him and her, attempting to drown them out. Forty-five minutes later they were still there, standing and shouting, unwilling to leave, lest the other side be seen to have won. Was it only Kupfer's postmodern dramatic flair that brought her into the fold? Time would prove that it was not: the passion for Wagner's music dramas was now something he and she shared, even if it had taken that production to make her realize it. Many *Ring*s later, he and she have read about these works, written about them, and still they are as fresh to them as that first time at Bayreuth. In love, the first time is always important, they say.

45

Henry James

It is safe to say that the great expatriate never had a Wagner Moment, at least not a pleasant one. James's (1843–1916) near-encounter with Wagner was the result of his friendship with Paul Zhukovsky, a young and attractive Russian, a dilettante painter, who introduced James to Turgenev, and, through Turgenev, to Flaubert. In 1876 he had dragged James to Wagner evenings at his studio, which James found intolerably long and boring. In fact, his decision to live in England was confirmed during such an evening on his last night in Paris.

Zhukovsky was an ardent Wagnerian who between 1880 and 1883 ingratiated himself into the inner circle in Bayreuth. His painting of the "Holy Family" (Wagner with his and Bülow's children!) hung in Wagner's Wahnfried study, and it was Zhukovsky who drew a pencil sketch of Wagner the night before the master died.

In 1880 James, at work on The Portrait of a Lady *and restless in Florence, decided to run down to Naples to visit Zhukovsky, whose villa at Posillipo was near the Villa Ungri, where Wagner was staying. The following passage is taken from Leon Edel's* Henry James: A Life *(1985).*

The Russian was all for James's meeting Wagner at once. The American, however, demurred. He had no desire to meet the "musician of the future," believing such a meeting would be futile—he spoke no German, and Wagner spoke neither English nor French. A flimsy excuse. Wagner, of course, did speak French, if not terribly well. The Russian spoke of Wagner as the "greatest and wisest of men," and confided to Henry that it was his ambition to go and live at Bayreuth so as "to take part in the great work." James doubted whether Zhukovski would do this, since he seemed such an eternal dabbler.

46

Speight Jenkins

*Speight Jenkins is admired nationally and interna-
tionally for his work as general director of Seattle
Opera, as a leading authority on opera, and as
an active arts advocate. In 2003 he celebrated his
twentieth anniversary as general director with
Seattle Opera's new production of* Parsifal, *complet-
ing the company's production of all ten of Wagner's
major operas, and also its move into its new performance home, Marion Oliver McCaw Hall.*

*Since Jenkins's arrival in 1983, Seattle Opera's productions have cap-
tured the favorable attention of critics and the public alike. Among the most
celebrated are his two groundbreaking productions of* The Ring—*the Israel/
Rochaix/Sullivan production that premiered in 1986 and the Wadsworth/
Lynch/Pakledinaz/Kaczorowski production that premiered in 2001.*

*Jenkins served on the National Council on the Arts from 1996 to 2000.
He speaks frequently on issues affecting the arts. He was previously a music
critic and host of the television series* Live from the Met *and frequently writes
about opera.*

I have three Wagner Moments to cite. The first was my introduction
to opera. At the age of six (February 1943) opera was mentioned in my
music class. That night at dinner I asked my mother and father what it
was. My mother said that it was where the actors sang instead of talked.
I asked if there was a story. She said, "There are crazy stories. There's one
of a woman put to sleep on a rock surrounded by fire, and her sisters fly

through the air calling out 'Hojotoho.'" I was fascinated and asked if I could read about it. My mother, who, like my father, went to opera for as much a social as a musical occasion, said that she would find a book on opera. It turned out to be Helen Dike's *Stories of the Metropolitan Operas*. She showed me *Die Walküre*. I read it and was entranced with it as well as with the stories of the other three operas of *The Ring*.

I heard about the Met's radio broadcasts and started listening to them. It was December of 1944 when I first heard *Die Walküre*. I can remember being transfixed from first to last. At that point I had started taking the Met's magazine, *Opera News*, and I saw the pictures of Melchior, Traubel, and Janssen. I'm not sure what this could have struck in me, but I was completely committed to this music from that moment forward. All I wanted to do, to my parents' amazement and despair, was to listen to Wagner—records or broadcasts. I attended my first opera, *Aida*, later that month and listened to other operas on the broadcasts faithfully, but it was Wagner that excited me most. My parents really couldn't fathom it, but I was determined and never wavered.

My first live Wagner was when the Met brought *Lohengrin* to Dallas in 1947. The cast was Torsten Ralf, Helen Traubel, Margaret Harshaw, and Deszo Ernster, conducted by Fritz Busch. I was ten years old, went with my parents, and became totally enraptured. I can't remember too much, but I know that I found it a transforming experience. It fulfilled all that I had imagined from listening to the radio and reading the stories. I can still see the swan, Helen Traubel in voluminous robes, and a vague recollection of a Swan Knight with a helmet resembling Valkyries of the period.

47

James Joyce

James Joyce (1882–1941) was an opera buff all his adult life, and his work was deeply influenced by Wagner's music dramas. An excellent discussion of this subject is found in the chapter "Comic Uses of Myth: Richard Wagner and James Joyce" in John DiGaetani's Richard Wagner and the Modern British Novel.

The following is taken from James Joyce: A Portrait of the Artist, *by Stan Gebler Davis (1975).*

Giovanni Battista Vico (1668–1744) was the author of *Scienza Nuova*, which had long interested Joyce, quite apart from the significant coincidences that Vico was afraid of thunderstorms and that there is a coastal road outside Dublin called the Vico Road. Vico's work had been the enunciation of a new cyclical theory of history. The cycle was Theocracy, Aristocracy, Democracy, followed by a *ricorso*: the Gods speak in a clap of thunder and we are back to the first stage again. The whole history of the world could therefore be enacted in and around Dublin and take place entirely in the dream of a Chapelizod innkeeper, one Porter, who is also HCE, and variously Humphrey Chimpden Earwicker (thence, via the French for earwig, *perce-oreille*, to Persse O'Reilly), Brian Boru, Napoleon Bonaparte, Finn MacCool, Parnell, Swift, Here Comes Everybody, Haveth Childers Everywhere, our Human Conger Eel, Hecech, and so on, through innumerable variants, many, no doubt, as yet undetected by Joycean scholars. To state that HCE has many identities does not make the detection of them easy. His wife, his daughter, and his two sons have also many roles to play. Chapelizod means "the chapel of Iseult," for instance, so the innkeeper's daughter becomes Isolde and Joyce is able to indulge a horrendous pun by calling her also "Mildew Lisa." The appreciation of that joke requires the knowledge that the first words of Isolde's aria over the dead body of Tristan, in *Tristan und Isolde* are "Mild und leise" (gentle and soft). *Finnegans Wake* is a gigantic multilingual crossword puzzle.

48

Benjamin Kamins

Benjamin Kamins has for more than thirty years been one of the country's out-standing players and teachers of the bassoon. He was principal bassoonist at the Houston Symphony for twenty-two years and has appeared as guest principal bassoonist with both the New York Philharmonic and the Boston Symphony.

Kamins has been a frequent soloist, performed the world premiere of the Larry Lipkis concerto Pierrot, *and has recorded the Mozart concerto with Christoph Eschenbach. A devoted chamber musician, he was a founding member of the Aurora and Epicurean Wind Quintets.*

Kamins is currently professor of bassoon at the Shepherd School of Music at Rice University.

I grew up in a Los Angeles of a different time. Actually, my neighborhood was West Hollywood before it became the chic, trendy place it is today. At that time there had been a tremendous influx of intellectuals leaving the antihumanist repression of Nazi Germany for the freedom of the United States. Ironically, many of them were the victims of McCarthyism after reaching the United States.

My father was a brilliant man of extraordinary curiosity and intellectual pursuits. He was a lifelong learner, and among his many interests was an all-consuming love of Music. His tastes were mostly limited to instrumental and piano compositions by the great Germanic composers of the eighteenth and nineteenth centuries: Mozart, Schubert, Beethoven, and their kindred souls. However, he had terrific taste in both the composers and the performers of this great music, and I have always considered him to be one of my greatest musical influences—even though he was not a professional musician. Wagner was a composer left out of these early experiences. It is difficult for me to know if it was due to my father's dislike of his music or revulsion at Wagner's anti-Semitic views.

Because of my father's many interests and restless spirit, he and I traveled a great deal, and there were constant trips to the many attractions available in the Los Angeles area. One of my favorites was the Griffith Park Observatory, a fabulous art deco building on a mountaintop above Hollywood. Anyone who has seen any old science-fiction movies or even some recent ones will instantly recognize the observatory, with its distinctive three domes and monument to the great astronomers of old, for it is a perennially favorite location of movie directors.

When I was about eight or nine, there was a Griffith Park outing to attend a planetarium show about the northern sky and the aurora borealis. This was in the days before computerized planetarium projectors, and the machine in the middle of the planetarium was one of those old projection devices that looked like a giant ant: two large round globe-shaped appendages attached by a sort of scaffolding in a sea of smaller projection units below. Of course, it moved mechanically by a system of motors, pulleys, and gears, making a soft whirring sound and giving the impression that it was alive.

The show lasted about an hour, with a lecturer giving entertaining astronomical information. Because this particular show involved a particularly vivid visual phenomenon, the northern lights, the last ten minutes or so of the show was done without words—only with projections and music. In this case, the chosen selection was the "Magic Fire Music," which concludes *Die Walküre*.

For a young boy, I was relatively knowledgeable about classical music for the reasons mentioned above, but nothing could have prepared me for the overwhelming effect of this grand and noble music—I had truly never heard anything like it in my life. I remember being particularly moved by the entrance of the leitmotif known either as Siegfried or, to some, the Heroic in Siegfried. It begins in the minor and ends in the relative major, conveying great mystery at the onset and clarity at its conclusion—the essence of Siegfried's character. Obviously, as a kid I didn't make any of these observations; they evolved with my love of this music as I matured. Nonetheless, the sweep and drama of the music with the visuals of the planetarium show (which could have just as well been a contemporary set for a production of *Die Walküre*) created a perfect operatic moment.

This was the start of a lifelong fascination with the music of Richard Wagner. Since then, there have been many other experiences with Wagner's music. Among them were when my high school humanities teacher let me lead the class for four days for an in-depth study of *The Ring*; the extraordinary series of performances of *Parsifal* conducted by Christoph Eschenbach, directed by Robert Wilson, with the Houston Grand Opera; and the performance of *Tristan* when the conductor's tempo was such that it took thirty seconds to direct the first measure of the Prelude—including the upbeat. So you see, there have been many experiences over the years—some profound, some humorous, all meaningful, but none as powerful as that planetarium show so many years ago.

Having been a professional musician for thirty-five years, I constantly search for the reasons that originally drew me into this glorious profession. It is a mysterious combination of talent, experience, and passion that sustains me through a lifetime in music. This early event was seminal in my search and helped to teach me how I learn and experience this transcendental art.

49

Wassily Kandinsky

Kandinsky (1866–1944) professed that music was a superior art to painting. In any event, his passion for music, and his intellectualization of it, clearly found its way onto his canvases.

The following is excerpted from Wassily Kandinsky and Magdalena Dabrowski's Kandinsky: Compositions.

The term "Composition" can imply a metaphor with music. Kandinsky was fascinated by music's emotional power. Because music expresses itself through sound and time, it allows the listener a freedom of imagination, interpretation, and emotional response that is not based on the literal or the descriptive, but rather on the abstract quality that painting, still dependent on representing the visible world, could not provide.

Wagner's *Lohengrin*, which had stirred Kandinsky to devote his life to art, had convinced him of the emotional powers of music. The performance conjured for him visions of a certain time in Moscow that he associated with specific colors and emotions. It inspired in him a sense of a fairy-tale hour of Moscow, which always remained the beloved city of his childhood. His recollection of the Wagner performance attests to how it had retrieved a vivid and complex network of emotions and memories from his past: "The violins, the deep tones of the basses, and especially the wind instruments at that time embodied for me all the power of that pre-nocturnal hour. I saw all my colors in my mind; they stood before my eyes. Wild, almost crazy lines were sketched in front of me. I did not dare use the expression that Wagner had painted 'my hour' musically."

It was at this special moment that Kandinsky realized the tremendous power that art could exert over the spectator and that painting could develop powers equivalent to those of music.

50

Alexandra Kauka

Alexandra Kauka is CEO and president of Promedia, Inc., which manages the media interests of her late husband, Rolf Kauka, who was known as the German Walt Disney. She is on the board of directors of the Metropolitan Opera, the Washington National Opera, and the Arizona Opera and is also a representative of the Salzburger Easter Festival.

I had long thought that nothing could ever top the sensitivity of Richard Strauss. Then I was invited to my first Wagner opera, which happened to be *Das Rheingold*. The lights were dimmed—there was complete darkness, and it was quiet as a grave. Then I heard that first tone. It was low, deep, and steady—as if a groan of the earth. It was the E-flat, which I heard with such intensity, produced by string basses. From this abyss rose bassoons, which gave depth, followed by French horns overlapping each other, producing motion.

This was the exact moment in which I knew that I had found music that expresses all that we carry deep inside us. The faint memory of creation itself. And from this first tone—that E-flat—I was mesmerized by Wagner. He touched my emotions. His music calms that unspoken fear of the unknown. He becomes an accomplice in your search for the base of your feelings, by painting musical pictures, which are all the more true because you feel them.

51

Winnie Klotz

Winnie Klotz is known to millions who don't know her; she was the official photographer of the Metropolitan Opera for a very long time, from 1976 to 2003, so opera lovers around the world have been thrilled and delighted by her pictures, with or without attribution. One of these reached a height of five stories on a billboard above Times Square. It is through Klotz that we can still see our favorite singers, and her camera always revealed them to us in their, and their characters', true natures.

Klotz took on unofficial but essential duties at the Met, too. Her little studio above and behind the big stage became the favorite destination, the refuge, for singer after singer. They all came to Winnie for hugs, psychoanalysis, reassurance, and gumdrops. She provided for all of them.

My first encounter with Wagner, after I became the official photographer for the Metropolitan Opera, was *Tristan und Isolde.* Some of my colleagues, I am loath to admit, some great singers whom we all revere, said to me: "When you go down to shoot *Tristan,* you better take along a good book!" I was undaunted. When I shoot an opera, I am totally concentrated on capturing that perfect moment that says it all. No time to be bored.

As luck would have it, on the first day of rehearsal the company was to rehearse the scene in which our star-crossed lovers really come together, and in which I would surely capture my perfect moment. The camera was loaded and I was ready.

The scene opened on a vast, almost empty stage, dimly lit by a pale gray light. In the middle of the stage was a small hillock, on which were Tristan and Isolde. As the music for the "Liebesnacht" began to play, the light slowly narrowed as the hillock rose and subsided. The light widened and the hillock sank until the stage was back where it had started. I stood transfixed, realizing I had just witnessed the coming together of two souls and two bodies—and I hadn't taken a single shot! But boy, was I hooked on Wagner!!

52

Evelyn Lear

Evelyn Lear is one of the most celebrated singers of our times. During her career between 1959 and 1992, the American soprano appeared in more than forty operatic roles and appeared with every major opera company in the world. In 1996 she won a Grammy Award in 1966 for her recording of Alban Berg's Wozzeck. *She also triumphed in Berg's* Lulu. *She is especially remembered for her musical versatility and was the only woman to sing all three principal female roles in* Der Rosenkavalier *at the Metropolitan Opera. She was also remarkable for her work on twentieth-century pieces—by Robert Ward, Martin Levy, Rudolf Kelterborn, and Giselher Klebe. Perhaps her greatest success was in the role of the Marschallin, first sung in 1971, and in her farewell performance at the Met in 1985.*

Lear has received a host of awards, including from the City of Berlin and the Salzburg Festival.

My husband, Thomas Stewart, sang the role of Amfortas in *Parsifal* at least fifty times at the Festspielhaus in Bayreuth, Germany, in the 1960s and 1970s as well as other opera houses throughout the world. Therefore, I was well acquainted with both the opera and his participation in it.

In 1972, at one of his last *Parsifal* performances, I attended reluctantly, not feeling up to par. As those who have attended performances in Bayreuth know, the opera starts at three o'clock in the afternoon. Then, following the first act, there is at least an hour's pause to allow the audience time to regroup and refresh themselves with *wurst* and *bier*!

I arrived at my row just as the lights were dimming. There was no applause (*Parsifal* is a sacred work and does not allow for feverish signs of approval), and I started toward my seat which, naturally, was in the exact center of the row (seat 25, to be exact, where the wife of the star is seated).

As I passed twenty-four people who had to stand as I squeezed in front of them (Bayreuth is notorious for nonexistent legroom) I received angry, disapproving, and unpleasant stares. When I arrived at my seat, I sank into the unbelievably hard, wooden chair with misgivings, but relieved that I had reached my final destination—and none too soon.

The gorgeous music rose and fell and filled my ears with delicious sound. The first act is rather long (what act in Wagner isn't long?), but I especially enjoyed the exquisite sounds of Amfortas. This was perhaps fifteen minutes before the end of the act. When the music ended, I was ready to leave my uncushioned seat immediately. But no! The people around me were so immersed in the religious aspect and the holy music that they did not move. I arose anyway and started to leave, again receiving disapproving looks. I tried to ignore them, although I did say "Excuse me, sorry, *bitte sehr, entschuldigen Sie bitte*" twenty-four times. When freed, I ran backstage to my husband's dressing room.

An hour later the second act rolled around, and I debated whether to make an appearance at my row or not. I decided "not."

The second act is all about Klingsor, Parsifal, and the *Blümenmädchen*, and Amfortas does not appear. I had seen the entire opera many times, and at that moment I was not in the mood. However, the audience was, because that act has all the hit tunes, exotic dancing, and suggestive sexual moments. I could just picture my twenty-four standees, with annoyed, yet puzzled looks, waiting expectantly for that irksome person to come forth. After all, this was the most exciting act of the opera and she would not want to miss it. However, she—I—did not appear, and I can imagine their even angrier looks when I did not come and they had stood waiting, as is the custom, for the last person to arrive.

After another hour, *wurst* and *bier* well consumed, the third act was about to begin. Of course, I waited till the last moment; I did not want to sit in that seat a minute longer than I had to. Just as the lights were dimming for the third and last time, I arrived. Imagine the group of twenty-four's furious stares this time! No "pardonnez-moi" or "excuse me" would suffice this time, and I had to look into their eyes as I passed—in Germany one never passes others with one's back to them; you must face them bravely and try not to breathe. You might get a whiff of bratwurst or beer in your face. But that's the price you pay for your disrespect!

The third act was performed fabulously. Everyone was giving their best. The orchestra in that hall was unbelievable, and the audience hardly dared to breathe after the last chord had died down. Naturally, I was so moved that I jumped up and was just about to applaud and yell "bravo" when I was poked in my back by a very sharp umbrella and given the "nay" sign. I was not sorry. I had had a great and moving experience, and the sounds of the singers and the lush orchestra, and the electric atmosphere, will remain in my memory forever.

53

Father M. Owen Lee

Father M. Owen Lee is a Catholic priest and professor emeritus of classics at the University of Toronto, where he taught at St. Michael's College for twenty-eight years. Though his specialties have always been Greek and Latin, especially Homer, Virgil, and Horace, he has taught over forty different university courses, both graduate and undergraduate, on many subjects in classics, comparative literature, art, music, and film in Houston, Berkeley, Chicago, and Rome.

He is the recipient of four honorary doctorates and several other academic and musical awards, and is the author of sixteen books and over two hundred articles. But he is perhaps known for his appearances, through the past twenty-three years, as panelist, pianist, and commentator during the intermissions of the live Saturday afternoon broadcasts from the Metropolitan Opera in New York.

If you had asked me some seventy years ago what my favorite music was, I would have said without hesitation, "Where or When," because in 1937 the harmonies in that song seemed wonderfully new and strange. But by 1938 I probably would have opted for "Love Walked In," especially for the harmonic change at the words "drove the shadows away."

In 1939 I'd certainly have chosen the song everyone was singing that year, "Over the Rainbow," with its arching melody and the brief, bluesy shift to the minor in its third and fourth bars. And in 1940 I might have favored "All the Things You Are," especially for the subtle and lovely key changes at the end of its bridge. Those were radio days and the golden age of American popular song. Month after month the new melodies came and went, each more beautiful than the last.

But the next year, all that changed for me. One Saturday afternoon, I heard my first opera broadcast from the Met, and nothing Richard Rodgers or George Gershwin or Harold Arlen or Jerome Kern had written meant to me what that new music did. That broadcast opera was *Tannhäuser*. Lauritz Melchior was singing, and also Astrid Varnay, Kerstin Thorborg, Herbert Jannsen, and Alexander Kipnis. Erich Leinsdorf was conducting. I can still remember the sounds they made. The music simply swept over me like a tidal wave. Long after the broadcast was over, the new, strange, wonderful *Tannhäuser* harmonies were buzzing around in my head.

I'd had about a year of piano lessons at the time, from the Sisters of Charity in depression-era Detroit. My father had bought a player piano for ten dollars from a Polish family who were moving and couldn't get the big mahogany thing up the stairs. With the piano in the transaction came dozens of piano rolls (with Polish words next to the perforations) and a huge stack of sheet music. After the broadcast I headed for that stack. I knew that somewhere in it was a dog-eared old book of opera pieces arranged for piano. And sure enough, there were several pages titled "Gems from *Tannhäuser*." I was just able to manage the shifting harmonies of the Pilgrims' Chorus.

What a thrill it was to have under my young fingers the very sounds that were echoing in my head! It was something akin to Keats first looking into Chapman's Homer. It was more than a discovery. It was a self-discovery. I felt that I had touched something that, however impossible it may sound in words, was a part of me. Something deep within this eleven-year-old music lover responded. It left me at a whole new level of awareness, astonished at the response that music could awaken in me. For years and years thereafter, Wagner's music was everything to me.

54

Oscar Levant

Oscar Levant (1906–1972), always quotable, once said: "There is a fine line between genius and insanity. I have erased that line." Funny, but perhaps true, too.

Levant's acerbic wit, displayed to the country on The Jack Paar Tonight Show *and in innumerable Hollywood films, continues to overshadow his remarkable accomplishments, not just as a concert pianist, but also as a composer. In the 1930s he spent three years in Hollywood studying under Schoenberg and producing a piano concerto, the First String Quartet, and the Nocturne for Orchestra. Young movie composers such as Alfred Newman and Franz Waxman were also in this circle. For the film* Charlie Chan at the Opera, *Levant wrote an original "opera." It ran about fifteen minutes and featured Boris Karloff. Reviewing the Piano Concerto in 1942, Virgil Thompson wrote: "His music, like his mind, is in touch and real and animated by a ferocious integrity . . . it is friendly and good music, all of it. It is even, beneath its trappings of schoolboy homage to Gershwin and Schönberg, hard and lonely and original music, full of song and solitude."*

Addicted, repeatedly hospitalized, and increasingly reclusive, Levant died in Beverly Hills in 1972. The following is taken from Levant's autobiography, The Unimportance of Being Oscar.

A writer I know was very thin when he started his analysis. He suddenly got very fat. Somebody said he swallowed his analyst.

Dr. Emmanuel Libman, the late great diagnostician, declared that lay analysts were Freud's revenge on the medical profession. And a psychiatrist in attendance at Mt. Sinai Hospital in Los Angeles said that a psychologist was to psychiatry what a chiropodist is to a surgeon. He destroyed my faith in everything I don't believe in. When I went into one mental hospital I never had any dreams, but I always tried to, just to make my psychiatrist happy. One of the unusual things that happened when I was incarcerated—a mild term for it—was that a doctor came to me and asked if there was anything he could do for me. It was the only time I recall any doctor asking me such a kindly thing. I thought of Richard Wagner and the *Ring* operas. In *Die Walküre*, Brünnhilde is put to sleep by Wotan for seventeen years or so until she is awakened by a pure young man who is, of course, Siegfried. I replied: "Put me to sleep like Wotan."

55

Claude Lévi-Strauss

Claude Lévi-Strauss, the founder of structural anthropology, is among the most influential intellectuals of the twentieth century. It has been written that "his extreme popularity (is) identified with his rejection of history and humanism . . . in his emphasis on form over content and in his insistence that the savage mind is equal to the civilized mind."

Also known for his structural analysis of mythology, he "was interested in explaining why myths from different cultures from around the globe seem so similar," insisting that "myth is a language because myth has to be told in order to exist."

The following excerpt is from Conversations with Claude Lévi-Strauss, *by Strauss and Didier Eribon.*

D. E.: In the "Overture" to the Mythology series you refer to Wagner and present him as the founding father of the analysis of myths. Did you wish to pay homage to music as an art—the four volumes are dedicated to music—or more particularly to the music of Wagner, thus alluding to a closer relation between him and your work?

Lévi-Strauss: Wagner played a capital role in my intellectual development and in my taste for myths, even if I only became aware of that fact well after my childhood, during which my parents used to take me to the Opera. Not only did Wagner build his operas on myths, but also he proposed a way of analyzing them that can be clearly seen in the use of the leitmotiv. The leitmotiv prefigures the mytheme. Moreover, the counterpoint of leitmotivs and poetry achieves a kind of structural analysis, since it works by shifts or displacements to superimpose moments of the plot that otherwise would follow each other in a linear sequence. Sometimes the leitmotiv, which is musical, coincides with the poem, which is literary; sometimes the leitmotiv recalls an episode that has a structural relationship to the one happening at the time, either by analogy or contrast.

I only understood that later on, well after I began my analysis of myths, and at a time when I believed myself completely cut off from the spell of Wagnerism. Let's say that I was brooding on Wagner for several decades.

56

Bernard Levin

From 1955 to 1997, most of those years with The Times, *Bernard Levin (1928–2004) was the most engaging, learned and witty columnist in Britain. Wagner was his favorite composer, and his repeated references to him became something of a standing joke in London.*

The following is extracted from an article that appeared in The Times *in 1988. It is difficult to imagine a more elegant explanation of* Parsifal, *or for that matter, of the possibility of Christianity.*

Over the years, the Wagner operas have rearranged themselves again and again in my mind in order of priority. *The Ring* (its constituent parts also go up and down in my ordering) stayed at the top of my charts for many years, but has slipped a little, while *Die Meistersinger von Nürnberg* grows and grows; to *Tristan* I go resisting all the way, only to be drowned full fathom five the moment the Prelude starts; *Tannhäuser* I wouldn't much mind if I never heard again, and I have never really warmed to *Lohengrin* (though I hope to hear Domingo sing it here in June even if I have to be carried in a chair, like Amfortas, or even in a coffin, like Titurel).

But *Parsifal*, which I took a good many years to understand (it is not a work for youth) and have not yet finished understanding, and never shall, now stands at the very head of the page, beckoning me at one and the same time into Klingsor's Magic Garden, which is death, and the Temple of the Grail, which is eternal life.

The contrast between Wagner's prodigious genius and his horrible personal nature has been discussed endlessly and fruitlessly; there's no art to find the mind's construction in the music. Some great artists have been of the most beautiful and loving nature, and some have been anything from dishonest to the most frightful swine. . . . Wagner, to be sure, takes the dichotomy to lengths unparalleled in all history (Georg Solti calls him *det old gengster*) but there is nothing to be done about it, and surely *Parsifal* is the greatest testimony in all art to the terrible truth that so enraged Shaffer's Salieri: that any channel, even an unworthy one, will serve as an aqueduct through which the pure water of art can flow from Heaven to earth, and not be tainted by the corrupted vessel that serves it.

There is a moment, some two-thirds of the way through Act II, when this lesson is driven home in the most violent possible way. Consider: the raging tempest of sensuality, which the central act consists of, is constructed out of musical materials very different from those of the two outer acts. This is reflected in the leitmotives that Wagner uses throughout the act; naturally, Kundry's dominates the list, together with those closely associated with her and her past.

When Parsifal enters, he adds strains from another world, and for a long time Herzeleide, the Wound, the Spear, Kundry's Wildness, Torment of Sin, Longing, Fool, and of course Klingsor weave in and out of the heaving, flooding orchestral and vocal texture. Suddenly, without warning, we hear, for the first time in three-quarters of an hour, the Grail. It is like a blow in the face, so enmeshed are we in the struggle between good and evil; but I never remember that it is approaching, with its glorious news that the battle is almost over and light has triumphed over darkness. Well, this time, when it rose from the orchestra like Excalibur, I thought it would stop my heart, so far had I been drawn into the furnace of the struggle. Surely this is what the shepherds who were tending their flocks must have experienced when the angel appeared to them with glad tidings of great joy.

The tidings in *Parsifal* are brought in Act III, when the Spear that pierced Christ's side heals the wound of Amfortas's guilt; even the poor production could not spoil that moment, so powerful and so complete was the spell of the conducting, playing, and singing. But the spell of the performance was as strong as it was because it served, with the utmost fidelity, the spell of the opera—its drama, its meaning, and its consummate ability to steep the whole evening in the balm of hope. And when you come to think of it, what is the Christian message but hope? Of course it is an oversimplification to read *Parsifal* as orthodox Christian witness; Wagner wove much besides Christianity into his final work. But if we generalize a little, we can demonstrate that the redemption of Amfortas is indeed the symbol of redemption of the world; remember that we hear, as Parsifal moves with the healing instrument towards the stricken man, the Grail, not Parsifal's own theme; and as the spear point closes the wound, it is not the weapon that sounds, but Amfortas himself. Surely Wagner is saying that Parsifal is neither the Christ nor John the Baptist, but the Paraclete of St. John's Gospel, who is sent to comfort the world: Peace I leave with you, my peace I give unto you. And it is man, sinful but capable of redemption, who receives the divine gift from the hands of the innocent fool, made wise by pity.

57

Michael Levine

Michael Levine is one of the world's leading stage designers. He was production designer for the Canadian Opera Company's 2006 Ring *cycle, which inaugurated that company's new house in Toronto, the Four Seasons Centre for the Performing Arts, and he also directed* Das Rheingold.

Levine has designed stage productions in theater, opera, dance, and film. He has staged operas in all of the world's major houses and is the recipient of numerous awards.

I have always found the whole subject of Wagner daunting and slightly irritating. All that high art praise scares me. It still does. I mean, how could anyone say that the *Ring* cycle is The Greatest Work of Art? Period. End of story. Oh, please. Isn't that taking Wagner worship a little too far? The works are long and bombastic and Wagner himself was, well, way too cocky if not extremely offensive. So . . . here comes my moment of epiphany. Okay, it wasn't an actual "moment" of epiphany, more like a very slow, drawn-out realization, which I think is more appropriate for Wagner anyway.

My work designing and directing the *Ring* cycle for the Canadian Opera Company stretched over a four-year period. I listened to an assortment of recordings of *The Ring* over and over. As I did, I gradually began to understand that using both music and theater Wagner was attempting to paint a picture of the human soul. What a noble pursuit. Worthy of high praise.

58

C. S. Lewis

C. S. Lewis (1898–1963) endures, as scholar; as author, especially of books for children; and as writer and lecturer on Christianity. In thirty years at Oxford, he led a revival of interest in medieval and Renaissance literature. Partly as a result of his friendship with J. R. R. Tolkien, he wrote works of fantasy—most popularly The Chronicles of Narnia—*to counteract what he saw as a dehumanizing trend in science fiction.*

As a skeptic and later a re-convert, Lewis explored popular objections to Christianity. Mere Christianity *was recently named the best book of the twentieth century by* Christianity Today *magazine.*

The following is an excerpt from his autobiography, Surprised by Joy, *which describes his conversion.*

The authentic "Joy" (as I tried to describe it an earlier chapter) had vanished from my life: so completely that not even the memory or the desire of it remained. The reading of Sohrah had not given it to me. Joy is distinct not only from pleasure in general but even from aesthetic pleasure. It must have the stab, the pang, the inconsolable longing.

This long winter broke up in a single moment, fairly early in my time at Chartres. Spring is the inevitable image, but this was not gradual like Nature's springs. It was as if the Arctic itself, all the deep layers of secular ice, should change not in a week nor in an hour, but instantly, into a landscape of grass and primroses and orchards in bloom, deafened with bird songs and astir with running water. I can lay my hand on the very moment; there is hardly any fact I know so well, though I cannot date it. Someone must have left in the schoolroom a literary periodical: *The Bookman*, perhaps, or the *Times Literary Supplement*. My eye fell upon a headline and a picture, carelessly, expecting nothing. A moment later, as the poet says, "The sky had turned round."

What I had read was the words *Siegfried and the Twilight of the Gods*. What I had seen was one of Arthur Rackham's of illustrations to that volume. I had never heard of Wagner, nor of Siegfried. I thought the *Twilight of the Gods* meant the twilight in which the gods lived. How did I know, at once and beyond question, that this was no Celtic, or sylvan, or terrestrial twilight? But so it was. Pure "Northernness" engulfed me: a vision of huge, clear spaces hanging above the Atlantic in the endless twilight of Northern summer, remoteness, severity . . . and almost at the same moment I knew that I had met this before, long, long ago (it hardly seems longer now) in Tegner's Drapa that Siegfried (whatever it might be) belonged to the same world as Balder and the sunward-sailing cranes. And with that plunge back into my own past there arose at once, almost like heartbreak, the memory of Joy itself, the knowledge that I had once had what I had now lacked for years, that one was returning at last from exile and desert lands to my own country; and the distance of the Twilight of the Gods and the distance of my own past Joy, both unattainable, flowed together into a single, unendurable sense of desire and loss, which suddenly became one with the loss of the whole experience, which, as I now stared round that dusty schoolroom like a man recovering from unconsciousness, had already vanished, had eluded me at the very moment when I could first say It is. And at once I knew (with fatal knowledge) that to "have it again" was the supreme and only important object of desire.

All this time I had still not heard a note of Wagner's music, though the very shape of the printed letters of his name had become to me a magical symbol. Next holidays, in the dark, crowded shop of T. Edens Osborne (on whom be peace), I first heard a record of the "Ride of the Valkyries." They laugh at it nowadays, and, indeed, wrenched from its context to make a concert piece, it may be a poor thing. But I had this in common with Wagner that I was thinking not of concert pieces but of heroic drama. To a boy already crazed with "the Northernness," whose highest musical experience had been Sullivan, the "Ride" came like a thunderbolt. From that moment Wagnerian records (principally from *The Ring*, but also from *Lohengrin* and *Parsifal*) became the chief drain on my pocket money and the presents I invariably asked for.

My general appreciation of music was not, at first, much altered. "Music" was one thing, "Wagnerian music" quite another, and there was no common measure between them; it was not a new pleasure but a new kind of pleasure, if indeed "pleasure" is the right word, rather than trouble, ecstasy, astonishment, "a conflict of sensations without name."

59

Jonathan Lewsey

Jonathan Lewsey, formerly the artistic director of the Mayer-Lismann Opera Centre in London, is the author of Who's Who and What's What in Wagner. *He is currently working as a freelance author and lecturer on opera and music. He lives in Cornwall.*

My first recollection of Wagner is listening to the Entrance of the Minnesingers into the Wartburg, from *Tannhäuser*, "The Ride of the Valkyries," and other "bleeding chunks," on a CBS cassette tape entitled *Wagner's Greatest Hits*. I was about ten years old at the time, and in bed with my grandmother on a Sunday morning, in her converted horse stables in Epping, Essex. Sadly I no longer have that particular cassette tape in my collection, though in all honesty I cannot say that this was a defining Wagner Moment. This was to come much later.

I say much later, but in actuality I had still only reached the grand old age of thirteen, when I discovered a highlights disc from the Philips recording of the 1965–66 Bayreuth *Ring* cycle conducted by Karl Böhm. This one disc was to have a profound impact on my life—an impact from which I am still recovering!

The highlights disc (which I do still have in my collection) consisted of Act I of *Die Walküre* with James King and Leonie Rysanek, "Siegfried's Funeral March," and the Immolation Scene from *Götterdämmerung*. At about the same time I acquired a highlights disc of excerpts from the Solti recording of *Die Walküre*, memorable chiefly for Decca's supersonic sound and Hotter's magisterial account of Wotan's "Abschied." But nothing on that disc prepared me for the all-engrossing presence of the Philips disc.

This was like entering another world. Something about the womblike Bayreuth acoustic so faithfully captured by Philips in those early stereo recordings, the chamberlike clarity of the orchestra, not to mention the visceral intensity of the soloists on stage, transported me from the tiny music room, situated between the kitchen and the utility room in the little house my parents owned in the village of Chelsworth in Suffolk, where we now lived, to the vast limitless horizons of Myth as captured so uniquely by Richard Wagner. . . .

Up until this time I had never heard a live opera recording, and from that moment I never again wanted to hear a studio recording—a sweeping statement—but it has remained true, and I have since only made an exception for the recordings of exceptional artists—Maria Callas, Boris Christoff, Leonard Bernstein—artists who would have made the air electric wherever they performed.

Certain moments in that Philips disc haunt me still—the ominous thumping of the timpani before "Ein Schwert verhiess mir der Vater," punctuated only by the audible creaking of a seat in the auditorium; Rysanek's rhapsodic singing throughout "Der Männer Sippe" and "Du bist der Lenz," and that extraordinarily visceral scream she lets out when Siegmund finally extracts the sword from the tree (this was an artist who absolutely had to be experienced live); the frantic close of Act I—has there ever been a wilder orgasm in music? (Surpassed only perhaps by the music of Brünnhilde in the arms of her father at the end of the opera); and then "Siegfried's Funeral March"—the apotheosis of those timpani beats in Act I of *Die Walküre*—and the call of Siegfried's motif ringing out with incomparable sweetness and dignity.

I wore that disc out, and it wasn't long before I had acquired the whole set of sixteen LPs, which henceforward accompanied me everywhere. That plush red box was my prize possession, with its lavish libretti providing copious images from Wieland Wagner's production, biographies of the singers, and most pertinent of all, long essays by the Jungian writer Lynn Snook, which put the work in a cultural context that began the process of explaining the inordinate sway Wagner's works held for me then and have held for me ever since; but nothing would ever replace that first magical contact with a whole new universe at the impressionable age of thirteen.

Bernard Shaw identified the age of thirteen as being the birth of the moral passion. For me the discovery of that disc signified that birth, or rebirth. Up until that time the biggest curse of my childhood had been boredom. With the discovery of that other world, represented by Wagner's life and work, there was no longer any possibility of boredom. There was only to be henceforth a long process of uncovering, of seeking out what it was that made that world, not just the sound world of the music, but the whole experience of the *Gesamtkunstwerk*, so alluring—by Thomas Mann's lights so dangerous—yet above all so compellingly meaningful.

The discovery of Wagner was my introduction to what Beethoven termed the empire of the mind (equivalent to Teilhard de Chardin's noosphere), which had nothing to do with the everyday world. The challenge from here on would be to find a way of reconciling this newfound empire with the everyday world in which we are all compelled to live. It is a challenge I've been attempting to measure up to ever since!

60

Saul Lilienstein

Saul Lilienstein (left, with J. K. Holman) is one of the country's leading analysts of opera. A frequent lecturer in the United States, he appears regularly at the Smithsonian Institution and for several years has recorded the Washington National Opera's companion CDs.

A student of Leonard Bernstein, Lilienstein has a distinguished musical background as instrumentalist, chorus master, and conductor. In 2005 he was presented the Wagner Award by the Wagner Society of Washington, D.C.

Awakenings

My grandfather had a pair of bungalows on Long Island. Each summer he would rent one of them while he and his family took up residence in the other. During the last week of June in 1947 we all moved in and began the annual oceanside vacation—and so did our new neighbors in the adjoining bungalow.

They were in the process of removing two large albums of old 78-rpm records that had been left there from the summer before. They had been told that I was a music student; would I be interested in looking at them before they were trashed? One stack contained the complete third act of *Die Meistersinger von Nürnberg*. The name of that opera was familiar because our high school traditionally used the Prelude to Act I as a graduation march, but with three more years before reaching the senior class I had never heard it performed. I stacked that pile of heavy records next to the Admiral phonograph player in our living room, let them sit right there, slipped into a bathing suit, and ran off to the shore.

The sun was too hot, the skin too fair, the burn severe. I was to be stuck inside for the next few days while everyone else had a good time. There wasn't much else to do than turn on the Admiral, and that is how it all began for me. The celli made their unison descent from the middle B-flat and then down into *weltschmerz*. By the time each stringed instrument entered I was stunned by sensations of sorrow and yet also of a warming consolation. Hans Sachs and his predicament were unknown. It was a pure music that reached me. There is a moment in our adolescent lives when the emotional windows are open and as yet unguarded by wariness or cynicism. If Richard Wagner finds his way in he can fill the empty spaces and will never leave you alone after that.

I spent most of that summer at the phonograph. My mother, a wonderful and sympathetic musician, found a score to the opera and gave it to me the next week as a birthday present. I was fifteen years old, stamping my name with an ink printer on every other page, proudly making the glorious music my own. By the time the summer was over, every note was memorized and cherished. I went back to high school in September as pale as I had left it in the month of June.

Was this the meaning of a life in music? This excitement? This life-fulfilling dream? A world parallel to the real world, in which all moment seems divinely ordered, where the good lives on and evil dies? Now nothing mattered but immersion in music, with some occasional time-outs for the New York Yankees and the unsuccessful pursuit of the opposite sex.

What kind of a school played Wagner instead of Elgar at graduation? Our school theme song was set, in the spirit of ecumenism, to the noble melody of Brahms's First Symphony. This was the High School of Music and Art in New York, an extraordinary place to spend four years, almost six decades ago. It had six symphony orchestras, two symphonic bands, and departments of painting and sculpture that rivaled conservatory training. Attending this school was like living in Hollywood's Fame but without the dancers and the rock and roll. The year before, when I was a freshman and still just one step from carrying a frog around in my pocket, the young sensation Leonard Bernstein led our senior orchestra in a rehearsal of Beethoven's *Leonore* Overture No. 3 before the entire school just before the semester was over. And then came the summer, that summer.

High school life was later climaxed by a competition in which I was chosen the most promising conducting student. The prize was a chance to conduct the senior orchestra in a concert to be broadcast on radio, the choice of music to be my own. I chose the closing scene from Wagner's *Tristan und Isolde*, the "Liebestod." I sank into a study of the score. Now nothing else mattered, truly nothing. The opera itself remained a discovery still some years in the future. Once again it was the purely musical experience that gripped me. From the clarinets that sang Isolde's first lines over continuous modulations in the lower strings, so tremulous and sensual, to the "resounding echoes" and "surging waves" of the great crescendo, it was not her transfiguration but my own that was at stake. There has never been a more thrilling discovery of the self and the greater world beyond the self than in those weeks of total immersion.

The concert date neared. A rude awakening came in the principal's office. He, a noted Wagnerian scholar, and my own mother were waiting for me. A decision had been made: "It was improper for a seventeen-year-old boy to conduct music with such highly sexual implications." I had won the competition fair and square. "Choose something else," he said. I refused. The second-place contestant took over, with a rattling good rendition of Bizet's "Farandole."

In the years that have gone by, I have been very fortunate to conduct that final act of *Die Meistersinger* and other Wagner as well, but the *Tristan* experience has always eluded me. The understanding of that vanishing moment in my own life has only increased my love of the opera, for did not Wagner tell us that *sensucht* itself, a yearning desire, is at the heart of *Tristan und Isolde*, and that we are promised no more than "a glimmer of the highest bliss?"

61

George and Nora London

George London (1920–1979) was one of the most compelling and beloved bari-tones of his generation. He sang a wide variety of roles, but for Wagnerians, his Dutchman and Wotan are especially memorable. He was the first American to sing the Dutchman in Bayreuth. His recorded Wotans, in Das Rheingold *for Solti and in* Die Walküre *for Leinsdorf, are important contributions to Wagnerian discography.*

London's career was cut short by the paralysis of a vocal chord, so he went on to other accomplishments—as artistic director of the Kennedy Center (1968–71), director of the National Opera Institute (1971–76), and head of the Washington Opera (1975–79).

In 1971 London established the George London Foundation for Singers, a grants program for outstanding young professional singers during their early careers. Past winners include, to name just a few, Kathleen Battle, Renée Fleming, James Morris, and Carol Vaness. The advisory committee has included many of the greatest singers of the past half century, including Evelyn Lear and Thomas Stewart.

The foundation is alive and well today, thanks to the leadership of George London's widow, Nora. The following Wagner Moment is taken from Nora's 1987 memoir, Aria for George.

Wieland [Wagner, Richard's grandson and co-director of the Bayreuth Festival in the 1950s] had the reputation of being difficult and abrupt [and] it was difficult to get close to him. However, he was always courte-ous to me, no doubt a reflection of the respect and feelings of friendship he felt for George. As I entered the auditorium for the *Parsifal* rehearsal,

I felt intimidated. I was about to sit down somewhere toward the back when Wieland spotted me. "Frau London, come and sit here," he said, pointing to the seat next to him. This was unusually friendly on his part for I knew he did not like people in the halls during rehearsals and George had to ask for permission to bring me.

There were at most ten people in the audience when the lights went out. I had the impression that the performance was given just for me, like for the king of Bavaria who demanded private performances of Richard Wagner's works.

Soon I was surrounded by the music, which I had never heard played quite like this. George wrote for the *Saturday Review*: "The entrance of the Knights of the Grail is unforgettable: from the deepest recesses of the vast stage, seemingly from infinity, an army of swaying men moves closer as the music grows in almost unbearable intensity until they have assumed their places around a huge circular table in the center." Then the Knights of the Grail intoned the Grail motif. The voices, chosen from Germany's best choruses, seemed to come from heaven. Then Amfortas was carried onstage on a litter. Instinctively I clutched my hands in a tight grip. Soon George's voice rose strong and moving, in his long "complaint." I was close to tears and shattered by emotion.

When the lights went on at intermission, I could not say a word. Wieland, perhaps aware of my feelings, turned to me and said: "Grandfather could not have visualized anyone greater than George London." He always spoke of Richard Wagner as if he were in the next room and would come over at any moment to give his opinion.

This rehearsal remains in my memory as one of the greatest musical and theatrical experiences of my life.

62

Laura Maioglio

Laura Maioglio is the owner of Barbetta, the oldest restaurant in New York that is still owned by its founding family. Opened in 1906 by Sebastiano Maioglio, the restaurant remains a fixture of the theater district.

Maioglio is married to Günter Blobel (see Wagner Moment 13), winner of the 1999 Nobel Prize in Physiology or Medicine. Blobel contributed his prize money to help fund the recently completed restoration in Dresden of both the Frauenkirche and of the central synagogue. The Frauenkirche, the largest Protestant cathedral in Europe, was the scene of the premiere of the choral work Das Liebesmahl der Apostel, *a massive choral work composed in 1843 by the Kapellmeister to the Royal Saxon Court, Richard Wagner.*

Laura Maioglio's Wagner Moment came at a 1951 Carnegie Hall all-Wagner concert. Here is a review from the CD of that performance, written by Dan Davis.

Sabata's Outstanding New York Philharmonic Concert, by Dan Davis

Die Meistersinger: Act I Prelude
Tristan and Isolde: Act I Prelude and "Liebestod"
Götterdämmerung: Immolation Scene
Parsifal: Act I Prelude and "Good Friday Music"
Eileen Farrell (soprano)
New York Philharmonic Orchestra
Victor De Sabata (conductor)

Oh, to have been in Carnegie Hall on March 25, 1951, for this all-Wagner concert. De Sabata was among the elite conductors in an era before outstanding podium masters became an endangered species. He's best known today for his classic *Tosca* recording with Callas. This Wagner program finds him on just as exalted a level. Despite sometimes harsh sonics that add an unwelcome edge to the brass and high strings, there's a remarkable combination of warmth and linear tension in these performances. In the *Tristan* Prelude, for example, the suspended harmonies at the opening lead to pauses charged with unbearable tension that make you catch your breath, and the tension is sustained throughout the piece—indeed, throughout the entire program. The *Meistersinger* Prelude is rousing, an exciting performance full of telling detail as well as grand sweep; the *Parsifal* excerpts are quietly intense, concentrated, without an extra ounce of flab yet never sounding lean.

The highlight, though, is Eileen Farrell's singing of the two great soprano scenes. Rarely do we hear voices of such amplitude and power wedded to such verbal sensibility and subtle tone coloring. In the "Liebestod" she enters with a voice numbed by the tragedy. Slowly gathering force and gaining in color, easing into climaxes phrased with such rightness and power that we can only respond with awe. Brünnhilde's Immolation Scene is equally overwhelming, Farrell singing with resplendent tone and focused passion. The New York Philharmonic in those days was a fickle bunch, notorious for wreaking havoc with conductors and playing that veered between the superb and the mediocre. Here, they are superb. De Sabata has them playing with precise brilliance, enabling his every intention to ring true. The CD bins are full of concert recordings best forgotten; here's one whose luster has not dimmed.

63

Thomas Mann

The towering figure of German literature of his time, winner of the Nobel Prize for Literature in 1929, Thomas Mann (1875–1955) and his art are inextricably linked to Wagner and Wagnerism. Deeply influenced by Wagner's probing exploration of psychological man, Mann also retained an objective, if not ironic, detachment, and so interpreted Wagner's art with penetrating insight.

Mann's courtship and marriage tantalize on both fronts, emotional and intellectual, subconscious and conscious. In 1904 he met Katia, the pretty and clever daughter of Alfred Pringsheim, a wealthy leader of the Jewish haute bourgeoisie *of Munich. Wagner was then as much in vogue with cultured Jews as Gentiles; in fact, Alfred, a distinguished scholar and enthusiastic Wagnerian, was one of the first financial backers of the construction of the Festspielhaus and a frequent guest at Bayreuth.*

Donald Prater, in Thomas Mann: A Life *(1995), suggests that Mann's pursuit of Katia was motivated to a significant extent by the attraction of the Pringsheims' distinguished social, artistic, and financial positions. Mann many years later revealed that his marriage to Katia was also, in part, a shield from his homoerotic struggles. Fantasy and reality may have provoked Mann's short story "The Blood of the Valsungs," the story of affluent and (by implication) Jewish twins, Siegmund and Sieglinde, probably based on Katia and her brother. Shortly before Sieglinde's marriage to a Protestant, Hundinglike dullard, the twins attend a performance of* Die Walküre, *return home, and consummate their own incestuous relationship.*

Mann's essay "Sufferings and Greatness of Richard Wagner"(1933) is among the best commentaries on Wagner. The following excerpt is taken from The Thomas Mann Reader *(1950), edited and translated by Joseph Warner Angell.*

My passion for the Wagnerian enchantment began with me as soon as I knew of it, and began to make it my own and penetrate it with my understanding. All that I owe to him, of enjoyment and instruction, I can never forget: the hours of deep and single bliss in the midst of the theatre crowds, hours of nervous and intellectual transport and rapture, of insights of great and moving import such as only this art vouchsafes. My zeal is never weary, I am never satiated, with watching, listening, admiring—not, I confess, without misgivings; but the doubts and objections do my zeal as little wrong as did Nietzsche's immortal critique, which has always seemed to me like a panegyric with the wrong label, like another kind of glorification.

64

Peter Mark

Peter Mark has been general or artistic director of the Virginia Opera for thirty years. During that time, he has overseen the development of the company—in each of its three home cities—now regarded as one of the finest regional opera companies in the country. In recent years, Virginia Opera has staged The Flying Dutchman, Die Walküre, *and* Tristan und Isolde, *ambitious undertakings resulting in highly praised performances.*

As a preadolescent boy soprano on the stages of both the New York City Opera and the Metropolitan, my fascination with the emotional directness of Italian opera and its galaxies of personalities brought me into the wonderful orbit of opera in a permanent and lasting way. Even the less flashy elements of Mozart opera caught my attention and linked with my own musical training and experience as a string player.

Having stood several times through the Met *Walküre* conducted by Mitropoulos, with Margaret Harshaw, I was aware even then that something unique was revealed by Wagner, which I certainly felt most palpably in the grand opening and sublime closing of the third act. But without a full understanding of the text moment by moment, I also felt it often (especially in the monologues that precede Act III) mainly in my feet!

In my gradual German revelation and conversion, which included visits to Bayreuth as a young man, I had gravitated toward Strauss's

Salomé and *Elektra*, not just because of their conciseness, but also because their power, eroticism, and imagination were more in tune with my hormones and metabolism as a young man. Conducting Wagner now as a more matured person and musician, I have fallen increasingly under his spell. I began with the tersely dramatic but totally inspired *Der fliegende Holländer*, then went on to savor every moment of the very human and epic *Die Walküre*. But most recently, I felt the depth, fullness, and ecstasy from which I never wish to recover, conducting the revelatory and multilayered *Tristan und Isolde*. Act III brought me to a sustained realm of beauty and understanding as close to the sublime as anything I could hope to experience, ever.

You see, for me, with Wagner, I guess it really was never just a "moment."

65

Thomas May

Thomas May began writing about classical music for The Washington Post *in the mid-1990s. His notes and essays frequently appear in the program books of the San Francisco Symphony, the San Francisco Opera, the Los Angeles Philharmonic, and the Boston Symphony. He is also a contributor to* Opera Now *and has written for* Playbill *and* Encore City Arts.

May's Decoding Wagner: An Invitation to His World of Music Drama *was published in 2004 by Amadeus Press. His most recent book, also from Amadeus, is* The John Adams Reader: Essential Writings on an American Composer.

As the Internet revolution was gathering momentum, May joined its ranks by becoming one of the first editors on Amazon.com's music site, for which he is now senior editor. His music profiles also appear on Seattle's NPR station, KUOW-FM.

When friends describe their temerity in the face of classical music, one rationalization beyond all others never fails to test my patience. They feed healthy artistic sensibilities with regard to the latest fiction, film, or gallery happening; indeed, often they proudly display their knowledge of important trends in the popular music industry. Yet suggest an evening at the symphony and they will react as if the notion of attending an up-to-date conference on string theory or nanotechnology had just been broached. Inevitably what comes back is the sheepishly clichéd excuse "I've never studied classical music and just don't have any background in it."

There's a reason this copout strikes a false note for me, and it has to do with my own Wagner Moment. Long before I first set foot in an opera house—or even concert hall—it became clear to me that music was destined to be central in the fabric of my life. Like others who grew up with Top 40 radio and the most minimal of "music appreciation" classes, I had essentially no background. Without warning or preparation, a series of experiences with no direct relation to my previous life overwhelmed me. They triggered something internal. Henceforth an insatiable curiosity was born: a hunger that, I inferred at the age of thirteen, when it began, would define large aspects of my being.

Summer is the time I associate with such moments of discovery: not because I knew anything about Bayreuth or other summer festivals, but because that is when I chanced upon the local NPR station (in the days when classical music was still one of its priorities) and began to hear a curious narrative commentary, as prologue or intermission, to accompany what turned to be a broadcast *Ring* cycle in progress. Just as when I had first heard the symphonies of Beethoven—that very summer—Wagner resounded for me all at once on levels that seemed physical, emotional, and spiritual. The music's beauty and significance were palpably painful—precisely because they made sense, yet could not be explained. What seemed most obvious was that this was an art reaching to the core, with the capacity to change a life. There was nothing pretty, or precious, or delicate about it. This was music that made one look within.

With the aid of a yellow plastic Panasonic recorder, I captured as many moments as I could. Lacking a stereo sound system at home, I took refuge in the listening room of my best friend's opera-loving parents, whose LP collection of the Solti *Ring* struck me as the ultimate treasure toward which to strive. Long walks, against the ebb and flow of cricket choruses, helped me digest what I had just heard.

Individual discoveries hover in my memory with Proustian exactitude—and in that paradoxical recombination of sensual, finite boundedness and the time-defying replay that opens, as Chekhov might say, into infinity. With the Prelude to *Lohengrin*, for example, I felt there was no way this music could not make sense or awaken the most delicious longings. Wagner became a touchstone for the rest of my aesthetic awareness. There were related enthusiasms, each new discovery increasing the joy of the others: the symphonies of Mahler, *The Rite of Spring* (my ignorance shielded me from the musical politics that would have told me Stravinsky was of an "enemy camp"), the fiction of Thomas Mann, *Moby-Dick*.

Could it be that every authentic Wagner Moment carries its antithesis within? My indulgence in his music—all of it up to this point, curiously, experienced via the technologies of mechanical reproduction—reached a temporary saturation point. I considered, about a year later, that it would be good to refrain from Wagner for a time, to explore other musical paths. And thus I inaugurated my own private replay and little drama of Wagnerian reception history, swinging from excess to ascetic detachment. But whenever I am ready to return and to lose myself in Wagner, I cannot escape this personal chronology: Wagner as the source of limitless discoveries that have just started opening.

66

Richard Mayer

Richard Mayer is the president of Ridge Investment Advisors, a Chicago wealth management firm. He has spent thirty years in the financial services area, thirteen years as a commercial banker and president of the Chicago Bank of Commerce and seventeen years in the investment management business with William Blair & Co. and Morgan Stanley.

He is also involved with philanthropy throughout Chicago, with a special project involving the Oscar F. Mayer Elementary School in Chicago.

In his free time, Mayer and his wife train and compete in local marathons and triathlons.

It was a beautiful evening in Chicago on May 26, 2006, when we crossed the street into Millennium Park, on our way to attending the final performance of Daniel Barenboim as conductor of the Chicago Symphony Orchestra.

The city of big shoulders said goodbye to an extraordinary musician and conductor on that night. He took Chicago's music to new heights. As his last gift to Chicago, Barenboim had selected his favorite act from his favorite opera: the third act of Richard Wagner's *Parsifal*. It was performed by soloists in the roles of the three lead characters, instead of as a staged opera. So my senses were much more focused on the music than on the story. I was able to concentrate totally on the notes and the individual sounds from the orchestra.

My Wagner Moment came at the very end, when the singing had ended. The soft beauty of the single last notes floated through the hall as if suspended. This moved me to tears. I was suddenly and profoundly overtaken. Clearly, I was in awe of the entire experience, in that moment. The tears could not express the depth of emotion I felt at that time. It was absolutely soulful and religious, as I felt in my heart I was experiencing total beauty. Perfection, possibly. Maybe it was God speaking to me through the music. It was wonderful.

It was the most perfect, most beautiful moment of my life. And I have that forever. Nothing will diminish that feeling nor take away the enrichment. What power to affect a person, a life, so profoundly. My enduring thanks to Richard Wagner for providing such a profound moment in my life.

67

James McCourt

James McCourt is one of America's most highly regarded writers of the last quarter century. His works include Delancey's Way, What's for Dinner, Wayfaring at Waverly in Silver Lake, *and* Queer Street: The Rise and Fall of an American Culture, 1947–1985. *His "entrancing send-up of the world of opera,"* Mawrdew Czgowchwz, *has been a cult classic for years and was recently republished.*

My initial Wagner Moment was not in the opera house but in the Polk Movie Theater in Jackson Heights in 1949 when I watched Joan Crawford walk into the Atlantic Ocean while over the radio John Garfield was playing a violin transcription of the "Liebestod." The picture was called *Humoresque*, one of Joan's many postwar single-word titles, all of which attempted to establish her as a serious tragedienne. Helen Traubel and Kirsten Flagstad recorded the role of Isolde (with the two Schwarzkopf high Cs in Act I). Martha Mödl, Margaret Harshaw, Birgit Nilsson, Régine Crespin, Leonie Rysanek, and Victoria de los Angeles (singing Eva, Elisabeth, and Elsa) all came in the 1950s and 1960s, but that high-powered sound-track moment (along with, I suppose, the Bugs Bunny–Elmer Fudd Wagner takeoff, but we can skip that one this time around) set my Wagner juices flowing.

68

Barry Millington

Barry Millington is chief music critic for the London Evening Standard *and the author or editor of seven books on Wagner, including* Wagner *and* The Wagner Compendium. *With Stewart Spencer he coedited* The Ring of the Nibelung: A Companion, Wagner in Performance, *and* Selected Letters of Richard Wagner. *He also contributed the articles on Wagner and his operas to* The New Grove Dictionary of Music and Musicians *and* The New Grove Dictionary of Opera.

In 1999 Millington acted as dramaturgical adviser on Keith Warner's new production of Lohengrin *at the Bayreuth Festival and subsequently on the first production of* The Ring *(also by Warner) in Tokyo. He is known additionally as a broadcaster and lecturer. From 1999 to 2003 he was artistic director of the Hampstead and Highgate Festival. His latest project is the launching and coediting, with Stewart Spencer, of* The Wagner Journal, *which begins publication in 2007.*

My earliest memory of Wagner is of me conducting the NBC Symphony Orchestra in a thrilling performance of the Overture to *Tannhäuser*. The rousing strains of the "Pilgrims' Chorus" remain with me to this day. I was six at the time. The recording was a 78-rpm shellac, and my podium, a chair in the lounge of my parents' home.

By the time I was fifteen I knew all Wagner's operas except one: *Parsifal*. I'm not sure how or why this had escaped my attention, but the opportunity to make its acquaintance finally came in a BBC broadcast. I tuned in on the extremely primitive radio I had at my disposal in the privacy of my bedroom and succumbed to the elusive mysteries of the Grail. I suppose some 50 percent of those shimmering textures must have been lost in the ether, but of course I didn't know what I was missing. What came across—and what I can hear to this day in my mind's ear—was the solemnity of the Dresden Amens and the chaste aura of that dubious community at Monsalvat. The conductor of that performance was Pierre Boulez, who had made his début at the Bayreuth Festival not long before in Wieland Wagner's second production of the work.

As a student a year or two later I subsequently acquired Boulez's commercial recording made for Deutsche Grammophon, but disencumbered myself of it in a fit of pique. Now that I had been exposed to the monumental interpretations of Knappertsbusch, among others, Boulez's fleet approach seemed intolerable.

Some three decades later, Boulez returned to *Parsifal*, conducting it at the Bayreuth Festival in 2005. Whatever one's reservations about Christoph Schlingensief's production, the conducting was superlative. I was intrigued to learn that Boulez's tempi for each act were almost identical to those he had recorded at Bayreuth all those years earlier. This great conductor—and history will surely commemorate him as one of the musical geniuses of the twentieth century—was decades ahead of his time. Now the fleet approach to *Parsifal* is gaining ground on the monumental and is arguably more in tune with Wagner's own wishes. The work is in any case multifaceted enough to be able to withstand such diametrically contrasting interpretations.

As for me, I'm still waiting for the invitation to make my professional conducting début.

69

Alisdair Neale

Alisdair Neale is conductor and music director of both the Marin Symphony and the Sun Valley Summer Symphony, and is Principal Guest Conductor of the New World Symphony. He was previously associate conductor of the San Francisco Symphony for twelve years and music director of the San Francisco Youth Orchestra. He has been guest conductor with orchestras throughout the United States and the world.

In the past eleven years, Neale has propelled the Sun Valley Summer Symphony to national prominence; it is now the largest privately funded free-admission symphony in America. Alisdair had a special Wagner Moment in 2006 when he led the SVSS and the soprano Christine Brewer in excerpts from Götterdämmerung, *including the Immolation Scene and conclusion.*

In 1994 I conducted my first (and to date only) performances of the Prelude to Act I of *Parsifal* with the San Francisco Symphony, of which I was associate conductor at the time. On the afternoon of the first performance I received word that the orchestra's assistant personnel manager had died tragically that same morning. She was hugely loved by everyone, and of course we were all tremendously upset. And as hard as it was to get through the Prelude while holding ourselves together, in a way it was very serendipitous that this work was on the program. Time seemed to stand still, and the mystical gravity of the score resonated with me in a way that I can't really articulate. But it was very real at the time—and the orchestra and I knew it without having to say a word.

70

Ernest Newman

Born William Roberts in the north of England and self-educated in music, philosophy, and nine languages, Ernest Newman (1868–1959) changed his name when he embarked on a career in musical criticism, seeing himself as a "new man in earnest."

*He worked at the Bank of Liverpool from 1889 to 1904 and did not publish his first book until 1904—*Gluck and the Opera. *From 1906 to 1918 he was music critic at the* Birmingham Daily Post, *and from 1920 to 1958 at* The Sunday Times, *as well as writing for many other papers.*

But Newman will be best remembered for his books about Wagner, and despite all the writing about Wagner before and since, he remains the starting point, and for many the end point, in this regard. Newman was the first to appraise Wagner's life and works critically, rigorously, persuasively, and so played the central role in separating Wagner studies from both the panegyrical and the demonized. As Father Lee has written of The Wagner Operas *(first published in 1949 as* Wagner Nights*), "Any Wagnerian in good standing knows it by heart."*

The four-volume Life of Richard Wagner, *considered Newman's magnum opus, took him nearly twenty years to write. In* Ernest Newman: A Memoir, *Newman's second wife, Vera, recalls the peculiar genesis in 1928 of that massive effort.*

At the end of May there was a story in the newspapers that was of great interest to E. N. Two Americans, named Hurn and Root, claimed to have discovered "documents worth £300,000" which would throw new light on the life and loves of Richard Wagner. The documents were said to have been accidentally discovered in the vault of a London safe deposit. They were alleged to consist of secret love letters, original musical scores, portraits, and the only known existing copy of Wagner's *Mein Leben*, of which only fifteen copies were originally printed between 1870 and 1874.

Philip Hurn, the discoverer of the documents, hinted mysteriously that they were collected by a wealthy Englishwoman who had determined to write an exhaustive biography of Wagner, but she had died before it was finished.

E. N. was naturally curious about all this, but he was not at all mystified as to the identity of the lady, and in his *Sunday Times* article of May 26 he stated that it was difficult to see how this mysterious lady could be any other than Mrs. Burrell, who had published the first volume of her Wagner biography.

Later Messrs. Hurn and Root published a book based on their discovery of the Burrell collection of Wagner documents. They called it *The Truth about Wagner*. This book so incensed E. N. that he felt impelled to drop everything and write a book in riposte, which he called *Fact and Fiction about Wagner*. This was published in 1931, and in order to write it he read not only the Hurn and Root book, but every other recent publication about Wagner that he had been able to discover. Being now in the flood of Wagner literature again, it was natural that he should go on from there to the big life of Wagner that had now been simmering inside him for some little time.

71

Friedrich Nietzsche

The intellectual ferment of the nineteenth century can have produced no more exalted relationship than that between Richard Wagner and Friedrich Nietzsche (1844–1900), dominant figures in music and philosophy, respectively, but also enthusiastic and highly informed amateurs in philosophy and music, respectively.

Wagner has been called the only true intellectual among all the composers of the greatest rank. One must remember that an evening of entertainment at the Wagners' meant a reading and discussion of the Greek dramatists or of Schopenhauer—or of the "difficult" essays of Wagner and Nietzsche. It can be said with some certainty that each man found in the other the most sympathetic and rewarding intellectual companion of his life. What we would give to have a record of their conversations!

When they first met in 1867, at Nietzsche's impassioned initiative, Wagner had already ascended to Olympus, while Nietzsche was only twenty-three years old, thirty-one years younger than the master. So they began as teacher and pupil, if not father and son. And their separation, for Nietzsche, was both inevitable and necessary for his further development.

But Nietzsche was as important to Wagner as the other way round, for he provided Wagner with the opportunity for conversation on matters of crucial importance and seriousness with someone he could regard as his intellectual equal, someone who actually understood what he was trying to say and do— a rare enough opportunity that Wagner craved.

The relationship sheds a favorable light on Cosima, too. Over the years, she was unceasingly generous to Nietzsche, actively bringing him into the Tribschen circle, and supportive even after he broke with Wagner. And it is clear from Nietzsche's point of reference that Cosima was no empty vessel, but a substantial and understanding intellect in her own right for whom both Nietzsche and Wagner had the highest regard.

Nietzsche's first Wagner Moments occurred while he was still a schoolboy at Pforta, where he and two colleagues had established their own "high culture" society. The following is excerpted from Curtis Cates's Nietzsche *(2002).*

A few days later Fritz went home for the short Michaelmas holiday, happier and seemingly healthier than ever. Most of these carefree days were spent in a wild "Wagner orgy"—as Elisabeth Nietzsche later described them. Gustav Krug had persuaded his two Germania colleagues to invest all of the society's funds in the purchase of a good part of the monumental *Tristan und Isolde* score (three times longer than Beethoven's longest symphony). Since Krug's father had remained a stubborn classicist in musical matters, it was on the Nietzsche piano that the two enthusiasts now sought to plumb the orchestral subtleties of the score. Having never heard a Wagnerian opera before, they kept losing the melodic line in an ocean of harmonic chords, though they struggled manfully to keep it afloat by singing, or rather bawling, at the top of their voices. Nietzsche, who by now had shed his earlier reservations, was so smitten by the *Tristan* score that he took it back to Pforta—to the dismay of his friend Gustav, who complained that he was being unfairly deprived of this "magnificent Wagner opus."

John Edward Niles

John Niles is the artistic director and conductor of the Opera Theater of Northern Virginia and also the program director of the Evelyn Lear and Thomas Stewart Emerging Singers Program, based in Washington, D.C. He is the son of the venerated Kentucky composer and folklorist John Jacob Niles.

When I was ten, my father, a passionate Wagnerian, took me to the Met to see *Parsifal*. My mother was horrified. She, a Russian-born (St. Petersburg) Jewish lady, was convinced that exposing an impressionable preteen to *Parsifal* would have a terrible effect upon me. She said that it would make me into a Roman Catholic or Nazi, or both.

She was wrong. I am an agnostic, a Democrat, and a Wagner lover.

Ignacy Jan Paderewski

Ignacy Jan Paderewski (1860–1941) was unique in the annals of art and politics, for having risen to the pinnacle of success in both. By the early 1890s he had triumphed in concerts on both sides of the Atlantic and had become the most admired pianist in the world. After 1900 he devoted himself chiefly to composition, principally for the piano, but he also wrote an opera, Manru, *which (like* The Flying Dutchman *and* Tannhäuser*) was given its first performance in Dresden. He moved to the United States in 1913.*

Social activist and Polish patriot, Paderewski moved to Paris during World War I and became the spokesman for the Polish National Committee, recognized by the Entente as representing Poland. In 1919 he became prime minister (and foreign minister) of Poland and represented the country at the Versailles Peace Conference. He subsequently represented Poland in the League of Nations.

Paderewski retired from politics in 1922 and resumed his concert career, but returned to public life after the German invasion of Poland in 1939, when he headed the Polish government in exile in London. He toured the United States, raising money for the Polish Relief Fund. He died suddenly in New York in 1941 and was buried in Arlington Cemetery. In 1992 his ashes were removed to Warsaw.

When asked what single score he would save from a universal conflagration, [Paderewski] replied, without a moment's hesitation, that it would be Wagner's *Die Meistersinger*, which he thought "the most prestigious effort of the human brain in the domain of art."

Tim Page

Tim Page won the Pulitzer Prize for Distinguished Criticism in 1997 for his writings about music for The Washington Post. *Before coming to the* Post *in 1995, he was the music critic for Newsday (1987–95) and a regular contributor to* The New York Times *(1982–87). He is the author and/or editor of more than a dozen books, including* Dawn Powell: A Biography, The Glenn Gould Reader, William Kapell, Selected Letters of Virgil Thomson, *and two collections of criticism:* Music from the Road: Views and Reviews, 1978–1992, *and* Tim Page on Music.

As a child he was the subject of the award-winning documentary "A Day with Timmy Page," about his activities as a preteen filmmaker. From 1981 to 1992 he hosted a program on WNYC-FM where he presented the radio premieres of hundreds of compositions. He was the founder of and first executive producer for BMG Catalyst and served for a year as the artistic adviser to the St. Louis Symphony Orchestra. He lives in Baltimore.

My first experience of Wagner's music likely came from one of the old Warner Brothers cartoons I used to watch on my parent's black-and-white Magnavox—Elmer Fudd singing "Kill da wabbit!" to the tune of "The Ride of the Valkyries," or some similar vignette. Later on, when I became interested in opera, the legend of the Valkyries enthralled me, and I spent much of my preadolescence secretly hoping that one of them (or her pretty, earthbound cousin) might swoop in and carry me away in her arms while singing "Hojotoho!"

But the Wagner Moment that, quite literally, changed my life was the day I sat down at my preferred listening station at the University of Connecticut Music Library, put on some bulky headphones that made me look like Mickey Mouse, and heard the Prelude to *Das Rheingold* for the first time.

This must have been about 1968. The word that year was "psychedelic," and I had no idea what it meant, exactly, although I had gleaned that "Sergeant Pepper's Lonely Hearts Club Band," Peter Max posters, certain books by Hermann Hesse, and the whole city of San Francisco were said to be awash in this new and mysterious quality. And then Wagner's depiction of the River Rhine began to play; a great, flowering drone filled my head; time was suspended; and I was transformed. To hell with Jefferson Airplane, I thought; this is transcendental music.

Much has been made of Wagner's harmonic restlessness—of the way that a work such as, say, *Tristan und Isolde* led directly to what has been dubbed the "atonality" of Arnold Schoenberg and his myriad disciples. But what astonished me in *Das Rheingold* was just the opposite quality—that is, the opera's unprecedented harmonic stasis, the manner in which it explores the churning, inner life of sustained chords, from the three amazing minutes of E-flat major that set the score into motion through the affirmation of the Gods, Valhalla, and an eternal D-flat major at the end. Put another way, Philip Glass can trace his spiritual ancestry from Richard Wagner as surely as have his more chromatic colleagues.

A dozen years later, when I produced a three-day celebration of what was then becoming known as "minimalist" music on New York's WKCR-FM, there was no doubt in my mind as to whose work should open the festival. Not Glass, nor Steve Reich, nor the young John Adams, nor any of the other fifty or sixty composers who were represented. No, it was Richard Wagner, with a single chord he had written more than a hundred years earlier—and nurtured yet another of his musical revolutions.

75

Jan Peerce

Jan Peerce was born Jacob Pincus Perelmuth in New York City. His first sing-
ing engagement was at Radio City Music Hall in 1932. Arturo Toscanini
heard the broadcast and auditioned him, and Peerce's wonderful fifty-year
career was launched.

But it wasn't singing Verdi that launched it. For more about Peerce sing-
ing Die Walküre *and drinking schnapps in the kitchen with Joe Bogash,*
and about Peerce and Toscanini, readers might refer to Wagner Moments 14
and 95. Striking evidence that Toscanini understood what Wagner wanted:
beautiful singing!

The following is taken from Peerce's autobiography, The Bluebeard of
Happiness: The Memoirs of Jan Peerce, *written with Alan Levy (1976).*

Audition at the Astor

Oddly enough, it was not as an Italian opera singer that I attracted
the attention of Arturo Toscanini at the beginning of 1938, but as a
Wagnerian tenor.

Editor's note: Peerce sang the first act of Die Walküre *at a Radio City Music*
Hall concert, which was favorably reviewed by the critic of the New York
Post, *Samuel Chotzinoff.*

Toscanini heard that broadcast, too. He told me later that what appealed
to him was hearing a Siegmund who sang the part with the proper

lyricism. After reading the review, he asked Chotzinoff—who was a consultant to NBC—if he knew me. Chotzinoff said yes, but he never would have dared propose a Music Hall singer to Toscanini.

"I'd like to hear this boy," Toscanini told him. He was looking for a tenor for a broadcast of Beethoven's Ninth Symphony.

Chotzinoff phoned me and asked if I'd like to audition for Toscanini. After I'd almost fainted and got up from the floor, I said, "Of course!" Not just at NBC, but in the newspapers, I had been following every detail of the great maestro's career; his creation of the greatest orchestra America has ever known; his escape from Italy by seaplane to Switzerland and then on to America just a few weeks earlier, when Mussolini took away his passport. I also knew about his reputation as an autocrat and I'd heard the joke around Radio City that "either Mussolini or Toscanini had to go, because Italy wasn't big enough for both of them."

John Pohanka

John Pohanka is chairman of the Washington National Opera and a director of the Wagner Society of Washington, D.C. He has for many years been the chairman of the Pohanka Automotive Group. He graduated from Princeton University in 1949.

Pohanka is one of Washington's most generous and significant patrons of opera. For many years the Pohanka Automotive Group has underwritten the WNO's opera lecture CDs, written and spoken by Saul Lilienstein. John is a keen analyst of Wagner's operas and lectures on that topic from time to time.

In February of 1946, at age seventeen, I traveled from Princeton to New York City to hear jazz played at Nick's in Greenwich Village. Walking down Broadway, I passed the old Metropolitan Opera House and noticed that they were performing an opera, *Tannhäuser,* with Astrid Varnay and Lorsten Rolf. Never having seen an opera, I thought that I would try it. Although I had no idea what was going on, not realizing that a synopsis was in the program—and of course there were no surtitles—I was totally carried away by what I saw and heard. Although I had enjoyed going to the theater, no theatrical performance combined so many elements in such a wonderful way, and it transported my psyche to a place unknown to me before. Bryan Magee best describes what it felt like: "a feeling of wholeness yet unboundedness akin to a religious or mystical experience."

When returning to Princeton I enrolled in Professor Roy Dickinson Welch's course on Wagner, and my continued study of Wagner and his music has given me some of the best moments of my life.

Andrew Porter

Andrew Porter is, I would think by consensus among his peers, and also among the artists he has evaluated, the consummate music critic of our times. His work, much of it written at The New Yorker *over several decades, can be taken as the most definitive record we have of musical performance since World War II. His reviews and essays convey erudition, candor, and common sense. He is also, among other things, the author of the most telling translation of* The Ring *into English.*

Readers are especially referred to Mr. Porter's essay "Richard Wagner—The Continuing Appeal," from the 1983 centennial reappraisal in Chicago, reprinted in 1987 in Wagner in Retrospect.

When I approached him seeking a contribution to this book, he told me that "although my life is Wagner-soaked, I don't remember any single moment worth writing about." I pushed, and he gave me these (as well as putting me on to Lord Berners; see Wagner Moment 12).

I had my Wagner Moment when my schoolboy fingers sounded *Parsifal* sequences on the nursery piano.

Another unforgettable Wagner Moment for me was the close of *Tristan*, Covent Garden 1948, as the lights closed to a spot on Flagstad's face and her voicing of the "Liebestod."

Marcel Proust

I gave a lecture on various Wagner influences a while back, including, among other things, the way Wagner stimulated new thinking about the nature of time and memory. This led me to propose, I believed in the spirit of common sense, that without Wagner, there could have been no Proust. My talk was interrupted by an emphatic call of "Nonsense!" from the audience. Imagine my surprise to learn that the catcaller was—Mrs. Holman, a dedicated Proustian!

In Marcel Proust *(2000), William Carter writes that in 1892 Proust (1871–1922) listed his favorite composers as "a trio of Germans: Schumann, Beethoven, and Wagner, the last whose music had become the rage among many in French society, creating a division between those who, like Proust, considered themselves Wagnerians and those who vehemently denounced this new foreign music. Marcel and his friends had discovered Wagner at the Sunday concerts they attended. Fernand Gregh, a schoolmate of Proust's who was later elected to the French Academy, described their astonishment as they listened, experiencing with each fragment 'the ecstasy of a revelation.'"*

The 1861 Paris premiere of Tannhäuser *produced a scandal that still resonates among Wagnerians. When the opera returned in 1895, it was greeted with ecstatic enthusiasm in a city now won over by new movements in art: Symbolism, Impressionism, sensualism—and Wagnerism. Proust, twenty-four years old, attended one of the performances and wrote about it to his friend, the musician Reynaldo Hahn.*

The following is taken from Marcel Proust: Selected Letters, 1880– 1903, *edited by Philip Kolb (1983) and translated by Ralph Manheim.*

I was extremely bored at *Tannhäuser* up to the solo. And in spite of the general cries of admiration, Elisabeth's languishing prayer left me cold. But how beautiful the whole last part is. I definitely disagree with you about the phrase "legendary rather than human." . . . The more legendary Wagner is, the more human I find him, and in him the most magnificent artifice of the imagination strikes me only as the compelling symbolic expression of moral truths.

Editor's note: Near the end of his life, Proust wrote the following passage with regard to artistic innovation and changing styles. It is taken from Letters of Marcel Proust, 1918–1922, *translated and edited by Mina Curtiss.*

Finally, you ask me about the "schools." They are only a material symbol of the time it takes for a great artist to be understood and placed among his peers, for the repudiated "Olympia" to hang next to Ingres; for Baudelaire, the judgment against him reversed, to fraternize with Racine (whom he, for that matter, resembles, especially in form). Racine is more fertile in psychological discoveries, Baudelaire teaches us more about the laws of memory, which, for that matter, I find set forth in a more living fashion in Chateaubriand or Nerval. With Baudelaire, remembering is static, it already exists when the poem starts. . . . Final and slight difference: Racine is more immoral.

As soon as the innovator is understood, the school for which there is no longer any need is disbanded. Besides, no matter how long the school lasts, the innovator's taste is always much broader. Hugo vaunted romanticism as his school, but appreciated perfectly Boileau and Regnard. Wagner never regarded Italian music with the severity of the Wagnerians.

79

Pierre-Auguste Renoir

Renoir (1841–1919) remains among the most revered of the Impressionists. He was working in Paris during and after the Wagner ascendancy. Renoir and Degas talked a great deal about music as part of the artistic ferment pervasive in Paris (see Wagner Moment 80: La revue wagnéri-enne*), but they did not like opera, or German music, or Wagner.*

But Renoir did have a Wagner Moment, when he was asked to paint the master's portrait in Palermo. Here are two accounts of that remarkable meeting (and less remarkable portrait), the first from Renoir: The Man, the Painter, and His World, *by Lawrence Hanson (1968).*

Before he could come back to France an unexpected commission was offered him, to make a portrait of Wagner, then finishing *Parsifal* at Palermo. It is difficult to know whether Renoir did or did not want to paint the man whose music he had spent so much of his time debunking in the Paris discussions with Maître, Bazille, at Lejosne's, and in his own Montmartre group. He seems to have agreed because an old Lejosne acquaintance and Wagner enthusiast, Judge Lascoux, begged him to. He was curious to see Wagner, yet when he reached Capri, he hesitated. Edmond, always anxious to advance the reputation of his brother, pestered him to do it. So "after having resisted my brother a long time I finally sent my letter of introduction."

It is difficult to think that Renoir was repaid for his efforts or that his reputation was advanced by what he did. Yet this was scarcely his fault. He began by feeling seasick on the voyage from Capri. At Palermo no one seemed to have heard of Wagner. When at last he tracked him down to the Hotel Des Palmes he was turned away once by the footman and put off a second time by Wagner's wife, who said that her husband had just written the last note of *Parsifal*, was suffering from a bad attack of nervous strain, and could not eat.

On his third visit Renoir was lucky; he was greeted graciously by Frau Wagner and her small son and, after being "plunged into an immense armchair," was eventually joined by the master "in velvet with great black satin sleeves. He was very handsome and friendly, offered me his hand, told me to sit down again, and began the most foolish conversation, punctuated by 'Hi! Ah! Ho!' half in French, half German with very guttural endings to his words.

"'Je suis bien gontent. Ah! Oh!' followed by a guttural 'vous venez de Paris?'

"We began to talk about everything—that is to say, I only had to repeat, 'Dear Master, certainly dear Master.' And when I got up to go he took my hands and put me back in my armchair. The nonsense I had to say, I blush as red as a turkey cock to think of it."

Eventually Renoir escaped, having made an appointment to paint the portrait the next day. Wagner said he could give him only half an hour. When Renoir arrived, the composer "was very cheerful, though he seemed very nervous. He regretted that he was no Ingres. In short, I think I spent my time well—thirty-five minutes isn't much—but if I had finished even earlier the portrait might have been more beautiful because my model ended by losing some of his cheerfulness and becoming stiff."

When Renoir had done, Wagner wanted to look at the canvas. "Ah! Ah! I look like a protestant preacher."

The one good thing Wagner had said during the interviews was a blunt, "You French take too much notice of critics." As for Renoir, he managed to sell the portrait to Robert de Bonnières when he got back to Paris so did not consider the time wasted.

Editor's note: This second account of that meeting, in some ways a very different account, is taken from Renoir, My Father, *by Jean Renoir, and translated by Randolph and Dorothy Weaver (1958). Jean Renoir was among the most influential movie directors in world cinema from the 1930s well into the 1960s.*

Lasco was later on to introduce my father to Wagner. Their meeting resulted in the well-known portrait of the great musician, and two or three sketches, executed in three-quarters of an hour. It was all the time the composer would spare him. They were done, I believe, in Palermo, therefore towards the end of the rue Saint-Georges period. During the sitting Wagner expressed opinions about painting that "rubbed me the wrong way. By the time I had finished, I thought he had less talent than I did at first. Moreover, Wagner hated the French because of their hostility towards his music. While I was working, he repeated several times that the French liked German-Jew music." Renoir grew annoyed, and countered with a eulogy of Offenbach, "whom I idolized. And Wagner was beginning to get on my nerves!" To my father's great surprise, Wagner nodded in approval. "Id is 'liddle' music, but id's nod bad. If he wasn'd a Jew, Offenbach would be a Mozart. When I spoke of German Jews, I meand your Meyerbeer."

Some time afterwards Renoir attended a performance of *Die Walküre* at Bayreuth.

"They've no right to shut people up in the dark for three solid hours. It's taking a mean advantage of you." He was against darkening the theater. "You are forced to look at the only place where there's any light: the stage. It's absolute tyranny. I might want to look at a pretty woman sitting in a box. We might as well be frank about it: Wagner's music is boring."

80

La Revue Wagnérienne

The attempted absorption of Wagner in France is a remarkable phenomenon in literary history; this was not just a Wagner Moment, but an extended Wagner period. It was in every way remarkable, not least of all in view of the residual, but growing, enmity between imperial Germany, victors in 1871, and the imperial ambitions of (barely) republican France. Even more astonishing, the French poets carried the banner of Wagnerism without having heard the Wagner operas! The French poets of the 1880s, heirs of Baudelaire, disciples of Verlaine and Mallarmé—Puccini's Rodolfo might have been one of these bohemians—as Symbolists, Decadents, and Impressionists carried on an unrelenting assault on the Academy.

The following essay is by Bet Briggs.

A French Connection

So appreciated was Wagner in literary France, that a monthly journal devoted entirely to him, *La revue wagnérienne*, was founded in Paris in February 1885. Its aim was to promote Wagner not only as a composer but also as a poet and the creator of a new form of art. The journal included translations of his essays and libretti, studies of him, book reviews, poems, press clippings, occasional lithographs by painters Henri Fantin-Latour and Odilon Redon, and also a bulletin of performances of Wagner's works throughout Europe.

Issued 1885–88, *La revue wagnérienne* was founded by Édouard Dujardin, poet, novelist, and disciple of Symbolist Stéphane Mallarmé.

Dujardin shared editorial duties with co-founder Théodore de Wyzewa, a French musicologist born in Russia of Polish descent, and English aristocrat and Germanophile, Houston Stewart Chamberlain, who married Wagner's daughter Eva in 1908.

The journal was closely associated with the Symbolists, for Dujardin was also founder and editor of the Symbolist magazine *La revue indépendente*. Mallarmé and other Symbolists contributed to both journals. Of Mallarmé's essay "Richard Wagner, rêveries d 'un poete francais," in *La revue wagnérienne* (August 1885), it has been suggested that it was "more the idea of Wagner that inspired his reverie rather than any specific work." For Mallarmé had had very little experience of Wagner's music until Dujardin took him to a Sunday concert.

A special tribute to Wagner in the *Revue* of January 1886 included sonnets by Mallarmé, Paul Verlaine, Charles Morice, René Ghil, and Stuart Merrill. Of these Symbolist poets Mallarmé and Verlaine are the better known. But Morice and Ghil were important theorists of the movement. Morice theorised in "La littérature de tout à 1'heure" (1889) "on the need for vagueness in poetry, for great thoughts to be veiled rather than clearly expressed."

Ghil, impressed by Wagner's ideas of the integration of poetry and music, propounded "a theory by application of which poetry was to become indistinguishable from music." In his essays "La traité du verbe" and "De la poésie scientifique" he expounded "the doctrine of 'l'instrumentation verbale,'" namely that the musical quality of a poem could be intensified and the theme orchestrated by the conscious use of certain groups of vowels and consonants as if [they were] parts of an orchestra. Merrill's poems "Les gammes" and "Les fastes" were experiments in versification and in orchestration of verse, very likely in response to Ghil's theory.

Other contributors were novelist Joris Karl Huysmans, who wrote on the Overture to *Tannhäuser*, English poet and critic Algernon Charles Swinburne on the death of Wagner, and Wyzewa on Wagnerian painting, supposedly inspired by the ideals of Bayreuth, by such painters as Edgar Degas and Gustave Moreau.

Wyzewa's essay in the *Revue* of June 1886 was an example of the journal's eclectic approach to its subject matter. His "Littérature wagnérienne" drew together such diverse novelists and poets as Huysman,

Émile Zola, Paul Bourget, Auguste Comte de Villiers de L'Isle-Aidain, Verlaine, and Mallarmé. In 1895 a collection of Wyzewa's *Revue* articles was published under the title "Nos maîtres."

Another erudite contributor to the *Revue* was Victor Wilder, Belgian music critic and translator and passionate Wagnerian. He wrote on the ritual of the *Meistersinger* for the *Revue* and acted as adviser on the first Paris staging of *Lohengrin*. Wilder also translated all of Wagner's operas from *Lohengrin* on. Cosima Wagner preferred his translation to those of Charles-Louis-Étienne Nuitter (an anagram of his surname Truinet), one of the first Frenchmen to appreciate Wagner. He, too, translated *Tannhäuser, Rienzi, Lohengrin*, and *Der fliegende Holländer*. Wilder's librettos were rejected by the fanatics of the *Revue*, who wanted those of French music writer Alfred Ernst to be used. Ernst, another prominent champion of Wagner, translated *Die Meistersinger, Parsifal*, and *The Ring* for French singing, and wrote books on Wagner and contemporary drama [and on] Wagner's poetical works, and a study of *Tannhäuser*.

The young founder and editor of the *Revue*, Dujardin, was a man of distinction, too. Described as "a dandy given to wearing Lohengrin's swan as an insignia on his vests," he was, however, a versatile writer. He published verse, "Poésies" and "Mari Magno," two volumes of *Théâtre* (landmark plays in Symbolism), lectured and wrote on the history of religious belief, and wrote novels. Probably his most notable achievement was his correlation of Wagner's use of leitmotif and the introduction of *monologue intérieur* into narrative prose. His novel *Les lauriers sont coupés* (1888) is an early example of its use, and was a direct influence on the young James Joyce, who later honored Dujardin as the discoverer of the stream-of-consciousness technique which he developed to its ultimate in his own novel *Ulysses* (1922).

Whatever *La revue wagnérienne* may have done for Wagner in its three years of existence, it did much to encourage public perception of the Symbolist movement. It also provided a stimulating environment and lively forum for the exchange of literary, philosophical, and musical ideas that Wagner inspired.

81

Kenneth Ringle

Ken Ringle was a prizewinning reporter, essayist, and critic with The Washington Post *for more than thirty years. He now writes from retirement.*

I was a reluctant convert. My opera preferences tend to be eccentric and highly personal, and to the extent I paid any attention at all to Wagner's music when I heard it on the Saturday Met broadcasts, it sounded overlong and overblown—musical bombast with at least one too many acts. I tended to buy into the stereotype of endomorphic Viking sopranos in horned helmets, shrieking to no good effect.

In the end, however, I was whipsawed. On one side I had an erudite cousin I much admired who had traveled the world, read every book, and seen every picture and play. He traveled repeatedly to Bayreuth and, despite his passion for the Italian Renaissance, boldly declared, without qualification, that Wagner's *Ring* cycle was the crowning achievement of Western civilization.

On the other side was his apparent opposite—a raucous, motorcycle-riding neighbor (he now owns a car wash), infected by Wagner while doing counterintelligence work for the U.S. Army in Germany. He, too, had been to Bayreuth and said experiencing the entire *Ring* cycle was the greatest artistic experience of his life.

So when the Deutsch Oper Berlin brought *The Ring* to Washington in 1989, I took a deep breath, bought tickets to the whole cycle for my wife and myself, and plunged in. All I can say is that, from that first deep E-flat of *Das Rheingold* to the last crumbling of Valhalla sixteen hours later, we were transfixed. The leitmotifs played in our dreams. We couldn't wait for each new performance. At the end Candyce looked at me and said, "I want to go through the whole thing again tomorrow. I can't bear to have it end." I felt the same way.

This was saying something, because the Deutsch Oper Berlin's production was designed around a "time tunnel" set based on Washington's Metro stations. The Valkyries were hallooing morgue-attendant biker babes in black leather slacks (not the most flattering garb for Wagnerian sopranos), and Fafner was a sort of doomsday mechanical dragon on Caterpillar tractor treads who expired in an eruption of sparks, flashing lights, and blown fuses. But even though I may have napped briefly at some point during "Siegfried's Rhine Journey," I was wholly captivated. I bought the bargain-basement Furtwängler recording and listened to Fricka kvetching in my car.

82

Rudolph Sabor

*Rudolph Sabor has been one of England's great teach-
ers of music for more than a half century. Among a
myriad of accomplishments, he is the author of both*
Der Ring des Nibelungen: A Companion *and the
delightful—and persuasive—*The Real Wagner. *He
lives in Petts Wood, Surrey, his home filled with one of
the most comprehensive of private Wagner libraries.*

It was the summer of 1939. A ship, the last ship before war was
unleashed, was crossing the Channel into freedom, to England. The
passengers were the flotsam and jetsam of society, some in fur coats,
others with rucksacks and nothing else, assorted spies and artists, myself
included.

A year later I was teaching in a school for the buoyant, many of
whom were later to be heard or seen on the concert platforms, stages,
or auditoriums of universities. Bombs were falling all around. A fellow
teacher invited me and a group of his pupils to his room to hear an opera
of Wagner on the radio. Among the singers was Kirsten Flagstad. It
was sung in German, the language of the enemy. We were devastated.
Returning to our quarters, I doubt whether any of us found sleep that
night. No, that was not my Wagnerian moment. In 2002, sixty-two
years later, I published a collection of my poetry, with the following
foreword:

> Strange and exciting, this encounter with hardly remembered verses
> from dimly remembered days. But here they are, bright-eyed spring

fellows, cathedral sparrows, portable cupids and suchlike giddy folk. Some is puerile, some is awkward echo, but all of it had been genuinely felt at the time of writing. Thus, I celebrate a reunion of basic emotions and experiences of my life.

And there, "in those dimly remembered days," that is where I encountered my first, the magic Wagner Moment. The year was 1932, the last year of the Weimar Republic. Otto Helgers, *basso profundo*, was the darling of the audience, and his son, Heinz, invited me to share his father's box at the Berlin opera house. We were thirteen then. But the bewitching moment, that mini-aria, in which Siegfried storms away from Mime into freedom has reigned my life. I did not walk, I ran home, grabbed pen and paper, and wrote the following:

> I did not expect too much last night at the opera house in Berlin,
> music of this kind and drama of that has never been heard or seen.
> The Woodbird's jubilant clarion calls ravished our eager senses.
> Brünnhilde's heroic defiance of fate shattered the soul's defences.
> Young Siegfried's voice, so clear, so sure,
> Sweet forest music, joyful and pure.
> High up in space a chord stands still,
> Resolves, reforms, abides at will.
> No master wrote this. It was a god who gave this music birth.
> To serve this god in steadfast faith shall be my purpose on earth.
> I will sing the way only he would dare,
> That the people feel they are walking on air.
> Folk shall forget their hustle and bustle,
> And thrill to the sound of the forest rustle.
> This joy must be felt by all the world.
> No greater dream was ever dreamed.
> Then would the people on this earth
> be remade and redeemed.

John Singer Sargent and Judith Gautier

The magnificent Sargent (1856–1925) was an enthusiastic Wagnerian, especially during the Paris years, when Wagnerism was conquering the sensibilities of the French aesthetes.

Judith Gautier (1850–1918), the daughter of the novelist Théophile Gautier, was significant in Wagner's life, both as persuasive advocate of his art and as partner in his final, surely platonic, affair, during the opening Ring *at Bayreuth in 1876, and as a focus of his increasing voluptualism during the composition of* Parsifal.

At the same time, Sargent, like Wagner and many others, was struck by

Judith's beauty, intelligence—she was an accomplished writer and critic—and liberality. He painted her at least six times, around 1883–85; at the same time he was painting Madame Gautreau (Madame X).

In the Tate's catalogue *Sargent* (1998), Richard Ormond says of this painting of Gautier, *A Gust of Wind*, that there is "no other impressionist sketch of (Sargent's) early period so daring in its juxtaposition of figure and landscape, or so full of verve and freedom in expression."

Christina Scheppelmann

A native of Hamburg, Germany, Christina Scheppelmann began her career as an artists' manager in Milan, Italy, and has since moved on to work in such respected opera houses as the Gran Teatre del Liceu in Barcelona and the Gran Teatro La Fenice in Venice, and as artistic administrator of the San Francisco Opera. In June 2002 Christina accepted the position of director of artistic operations for the Washington National Opera. Since then she, in coordination with gen-eral director Plácido Domingo, has planned and prepared all artistic aspects of the WNO and has helped to advance the WNO's reputation as a world-class opera company.

It is hard for me to choose my very best Wagner Moment, but I will never forget the first one. I was, at that time, about fifteen years old and was singing in the children's chorus of the Hamburg State Opera. We were going to perform *Parsifal*, and the conductor was the wonder-ful Heinz Fricke (still conducting magnificently today). During the "Transformation Music" in Act I, as part of the chorus from the height of the *obersten Höhe*, I was high up in the theater's second fly floor, and even while singing I couldn't stop watching what was happening below—the set and scenery all in glorious reds and maroons (designed by the Viennese artist Ernst Fuchs). I was thrilled by the entrance of the knights and their fantastic music, and by Amfortas's startling monologue.

I didn't really have a clue as to what was going on, but found the music and stage action totally spellbinding!

85

Iain Scott

Iain Scott is one of Canada's most popular opera educators. He has appeared for over twenty years as a radio commentator and quiz panelist on the Canadian Broadcasting Corporation's Saturday Afternoon at the Opera *and for nine years was a guest on the* Texaco Opera Quiz *from the Met. He is in great demand as a speaker at the University of Toronto and at Wagner societies and opera guilds across Canada and the United States.*

Scott delivers opera appreciation courses and conducts highly popular opera tours through his company OPERA-IS, www.opera-is.com.

I had been waiting for half an hour and was just on the point of giving up—when he appeared, disheveled and gloomy. "I am no longer interested in helping you prepare for your presentation tomorrow," he said. "Stay if you like, or go." Clueless about reading hints, I stayed. He poured himself three fingers of scotch. Even to this day I remember my feelings of resentment when he did not offer me any. He closed the curtains and put on a 45-rpm record. We listened in the dark. He played it again. Then a third time.

"Do you want to talk about it?" Silence. I knew that he was a Samaritan, a face-to-face suicide volunteer, and wondered if perhaps he had just returned from an unsuccessful intervention. I never discovered what "it" had been. But we did talk. Well into the wee hours of the night, we talked about that record. Not about why he had played it, but about the safer topics of who and what. Who was this Kirsten Flagstad? What was she singing about? And who was Isolde?

That was the night I discovered the profundity, the potential and the power of Wagner. A whole new world opened up for me. No one has ever expressed the stunning joy of discovery more sublimely than John Keats: "Then felt I like some watcher of the skies when a new planet swims into his ken." I was equally ecstatic and exhilarated. As awestruck and stunned as stout Cortés and his men had been on that peak in Darien, I was overwhelmed by the prospect of how much there was to learn.

As a postscript to this epiphany, an early experience on my exploratory journey provided me with a second shock. My first baby step had been a mistake. I had gone to see a *Parsifal* and had found Gurnemanz, in particular, to be incomprehensible, interminable, and tiresome. Everything my friends had told me about the turgidness and torpidity of Wagner appeared to be validated. With some trepidation, a few weeks later I decided to give Wagner one more chance and ventured to see my first *Walküre*. In those days before surtitles, the first act was largely a blur, but I remember responding to the surging sweep of the love duet just before the curtain fell. In the middle of the second act, however, the stage lighting gradually lowered to focus on an old man monotonously droning on to his daughter. The texture of the orchestra imperceptibly descended and dissipated. By the time it was down to a single double bass, I had been comfortably conveyed to the exquisite Land of Nod. I was roused from my bliss by the applause at the end of the act. What *Todesverkundigung*? What battle?

My second shattering Wagner epiphany came when I read a subsequent newspaper review of that performance. "In thirty years as a critic," he wrote, "I have never seen or heard Wotan's second-act narration more movingly and insightfully sung than by Hans Hotter at Covent Garden last night. This crucial scene burned with such incandescent intensity that it proved without a doubt why it is the most central and revelatory moment of the entire *Ring* cycle." Wow—and I had just slept right through it! Clearly, there was so much that I needed to learn! But, equally incontestably, this journey of discovery was going to be ultimately rewarding!

Editor's note: For an account of Hotter's approach to the Wotan narration, see Wagner Moment 42.

86

George Bernard Shaw and Alfred Turco

Having failed in my search for Shaw's Wagner Moment, I turned to Alfred Turco, an acknowledged Shaw expert, the author of The Perfect Wagnerite. *Alfred Turco attended Brown and Harvard before joining the faculty of Wesleyan University in 1967, where he has taught dramatic literature—including opera—ever since. The author of* Shaw's Moral Vision *(1976), he has written also on Ibsen, Strindberg, Nietzsche, and—inevitably—the creator of the* Ring *cycle. His own Wagner Moment having apparently been prenatal, Turco here reconstructs that of his favorite dramatist.*

"I was brought up on music"
—George Bernard Shaw

The Search for Shaw's Wagner Moment

Born on July 26, 1856, to an alcoholic father and an inattentive mother who was a professional mezzo and singing teacher, George Shaw spent his earliest years in a Dublin household permeated by the sounds of music. The repertory of rehearsals and musicales consisted in large part of Italian opera (Donizetti, Verdi, Mozart) and German oratorio (Bach, Handel, Mendelssohn). The boy's favorite opera was *Faust*. Literature and music were his only stimulation: in 1871 he left school for the last (though not the first) time to begin a dreary "office-boyhood" that stretched to four and a half years.

Long afterward Shaw recollected that "Wagner did not exist for us" during the 1860s. His "Wagner Moment"—if so precise a phrase fits— must have come later. Surely by the time "Corno di Bassetto" became chief music critic for *The Star* in 1889, he was a confirmed Wagnerian if not quite yet a "Wagnerite." From this *terminus ante quem*, how far back can we go?

Eighteen-eighty-three? William Archer, Ibsen's first English translator, notices a young man in the British Museum's Reading Room, "with pallid skin and bright red hair and beard . . . day after day poring over Karl Marx's *Das Kapital* and an orchestral score of Wagner's *Tristan und Isolde*." A momentous occasion indeed—but the image (nearly iconic in force) suggests one already immersed in Wagner's music, not a new acolyte. In Cashel Byron's *Profession*, a novel written only a year earlier, Shaw's pugilist hero regales an audience by launching into a defense of "a man in the musical line named Wagner, who is what you might call a game sort of composer—he wins his fights"!

Eighteen-seventy-seven? Soon after immigrating to London on March 31, 1876, Shaw earns his first fees by ghostwriting weekly reviews of concerts for *The Hornet*. In April 1877 he notes an impending visit by Wagner—calling him "the greatest of modern composers"—to conduct a series of concerts in London. There follows a discussion—emphasizing *Lohengrin* as "the first opera in which Wagner is all himself"—of why the British have been slow to warm to Wagnerian opera. The fledgling critic's own warmth does not yet extend to the mature music dramas, which are alleged to "grievously lack . . . human interest"—a startling disclaimer in view of Shaw's subsequent notoriety as a *Ring* advocate.

Eighteen-seventy-four and -seventy-five! After his mother's removal to London in June 1873 to pursue her musical fortunes, the dull days in Dublin were intellectually enlivened by friendship with a lodger in the boardinghouse to which Shaw and his father repaired in the following year. Chichester Bell, a cousin of the telephone's inventor, was a medical pathologist, chemical scientist, ardent Germanophile, and musician sufficiently accomplished to contribute an article to the first edition of *Grove's Dictionary*. Of him Shaw writes: "It was Bell who made me take

Wagner seriously. I had heard nothing of his except the *Tannhäuser* march played by a second-rate military band; and my only comment was that the second theme was a weak imitation of a famous air, made up of a chain of turns, in Weber's *Freischütz* Overture. When I found that Bell regarded Wagner as a great composer, I bought a vocal score of *Lohengrin*: the only sample to be had at the Dublin music shops. The first few bars completely converted me."

Here then is the *terminus ad quo*—an earned epiphany traceable to his late teens—for the critic turned playwright who would go on to publish *The Perfect Wagnerite* in 1898. To this day Shaw's analysis of *The Ring* as political allegory remains both controversial and unkillable. Because he continued to comment pointedly on Wagner's music to the end of his life, it is clear that the "moment" had staying power!

Worth bearing in mind, however, is that "the Master" (a moniker Shaw smiled at) never displaced Mozart in his heart of hearts. When his mother packed her bags, the future GBS (now dreading a successful career in business) learned to make his own music on the piano she had left behind. Shaw describes how it took him ten minutes to arrange his fingers on the opening D-minor chord of *Don Giovanni*—the work which in his ninety-fifth year he still revered as "the greatest opera in the world." Bernard Shaw died on November 2, 1950.

Beverly Sills

Beverly Sills is firmly ensconced in the highest rank of American opera singers of the postwar era. Esteemed as a surpassing lyric coloratura, she was as highly regarded for her dramatic interpretations and for expanding her repertoire into heavier roles. Her successes onstage were matched by other accomplishments as general director of the New York City Opera, as chairman of Lincoln Center, as a driving force in arts and charitable causes, and as a mother and wife.

The following description of Sills's brief, and unfortunate, encounter with Wagner is provided by her friend and manager, Edgar Vincent.

Beverly Sills never sang Wagner, with one exception. That was at the beginning of her career, at the San Francisco Opera, where, among other duties, she was understudy to one of the multiple Valkyries in *Die Walküre*. Because the soprano whom she was covering took suddenly ill, Ms. Sills was pushed into her costume and helmet and shoved on stage. The result was that she lost the helmet in the middle of the "Hojotoho!" in full view of the audience. To make matters worse, she was trying to retrieve the helmet, to the great amusement of the audience, and thus learned a lesson—never to pick up something you have dropped by accident.

Georg Solti

I suspect that there are very many people for whom the Wagner Moment may have been exposure to The Ring *recorded on Decca by Georg Solti (1912–1997). Certainly it was for me. Most of what I think I know about* The Ring *is a result of a rather total immersion into those discs in 1968, with just earphones and the vocal scores.*

The Solti recording remains the most honored in history. Each opera, issued between 1958 and 1966, won the award for the best recording of the year, and the Götterdämmerung *is still regarded by many as the best opera recording ever.*

Highlights of Solti's career include music directorships at Covent Garden (1961–71) and the Chicago Symphony Orchestra (1969–91). He called his association with the CSO "the happiest time of my professional life."

The following is taken from his Memoirs, *published in same year of his sudden death.*

Before the *Ring* project made Wagner one of the central figures in my musical life, I had conducted only five of his ten frequently performed operas. During my years as a *répétiteur* in Budapest, I had worked on the early operas and *Tristan* and *Walküre*, but not on the other *Ring* operas or *Die Meistersinger* or *Parsifal*. I do not recall being either particularly pro-Wagner or particularly anti-Wagner at the time. Gradually, I conducted all of his main works, starting with my first *Walküre* in Munich, in 1947.

Emil Preetorius, the great German stage designer who had worked at the Bayreuth Festival, and who designed my Frankfurt *Tristan*, once described to me Wagner's color schemes, using examples that he played on the piano. The color that Preetorius saw, Wagner had composed in musical terms. Preetorius described the incredible variety of color in the operas—the blue of the *Lohengrin* Prelude, for instance—and he spoke about the color scheme that Wagner transferred into his orchestration. He told me that each Wagner opera has its own color. *Dutchman*, for instance, is very dark, *Tannhäuser* is a little brighter, and *Lohengrin* is silver—lots of A major, which is the brightest key of all. *The Ring*'s "color scheme" is extremely varied but basically dark; *Tristan* is multicolored, built on chromatic scales and half tones, while *Meistersinger* is in very bright, full tones—a diatonic miracle. This variety in color translates itself into an incredible variety in character, which comes across immediately in the various orchestral introductions, before a single note has been sung. Think of the storm in *The Flying Dutchman* Overture, the "Pilgrims' Hymn" in the *Tannhäuser* Overture, the otherworldliness of the *Lohengrin* Prelude, and the fatal lovesickness of the *Tristan* Prelude; or the atmospheric and seemingly eternal E-flat at the beginning of *Das Rheingold*, the terror of *Die Walküre*'s opening pages, the joyous playfulness of the *Meistersinger* Prelude, and the mysticism of the *Parsifal* Prelude. Compare the passionate Prelude to Act III of *Lohengrin* with the melancholy warmth of the Prelude to Act III of *Meistersinger*; or with the sylvan introduction to *Siegfried*.

Today we tend to look too much into the psychological motivation and character defects of the great composers at the expense of really listening to the music. I am not interested in Wagner's political or philosophical ideas, or his betrayal of friends, including his father-in-law, Franz Liszt. What interests me is the creation of his music; for example, the love motif of *Tristan*, the miracle and completeness of the first four bars, now regarded as a bible of love and beauty. I understand that he wrote several versions before this motif appeared—a harmonic and melodic miracle. To me, anybody who can create such beauty, whether he be half-Jewish, anti-Semite, revolutionary, liberal, or royalist, is first and foremost a musical genius and will remain so as long as our civilization lasts.

89

Frederic Spotts

Wagnerians are grateful to Frederic Spotts for his highly regarded Bayreuth: A History of the Wagner Festival, *published in 1994. The book has won numerous awards, including the Royal Philharmonic Society Award for the best music book of 1994, and is considered the definitive Bayreuth history in English. Frederic Spotts, after a distinguished career in the U. S. Foreign Service, was an associate of the Center for European Studies at Harvard. He now lives in France.*

In my case there was no single magic Wagner Moment—or, if so, I was so young that it has vanished from my memory. I can establish, though, that by the age of fourteen I was already a devout Wagnerite (also, it must be said, an equally devout Mozartite) and never missed a Saturday afternoon Met broadcast of any of the Master's works. But if there was no one Moment, there were unforgettable moments, and these occurred at Wieland Wagner's productions at Bayreuth in the 1950s and 1960s.

Precise memories of feelings are rare but I can remember, as if yesterday, my exact emotions on seeing and hearing the final scene of his first *Tannhäuser*, Klingsor in his sinister web, the opening scene of his first *Meistersinger*, and the second act of *Tristan*. But no other single moment ever quite took my breath away as when the curtain rose on the Meadow Scene of *Meistersinger*. Deep down I believe the impulse that inspired me to write a history of the Bayreuth Festival was a desire to repay Wieland Wagner for the greatest aesthetic moments in my life.

90

Jason Stearns

Jason Stearns is a bass-baritone who has sung in opera houses throughout the United States. For many years he sang in the U.S. Army Band Chorus. He has been a featured singer in the Evelyn Lear and Thomas Stewart Emerging Singers Program, which is committed to helping American singers with the potential for careers singing Wagner.

I suppose my first Wagner Moment actually was not a single experience for me, but rather one that came to me in a few stages. Perhaps because there are so many great moments in Wagner, one encounter is just not enough to get the big "Aha!" in one hearing. When just a freshman at the Eastman School of Music, I was given the famous recording of the first act of *Die Walküre* that features Lauritz Melchior, Lotte Lehman, and Emanuel List. The teacher who lent me this recording warned me that it would change my life forever.

I did a little homework first so that I would know what was happening dramatically in this first act of what is arguably the greatest music ever written. Sitting on my bunk bed with headphones on and a score of the opera in my hand, transported, I was suddenly running desperately through a dark forest when I came upon a rude home nestled around this huge tree. I fell, exhausted, on the hearth, only to be revived by this beautiful and sad woman who seemed overly curious about me. As we gazed into each other's eyes, suddenly her horrible, dirty, smelly husband returned and began making threatening gestures and remarks to me, while muttering under his breath that I resembled his young wife. Warning me to be ready for battle in the morning, he retired, but she soon returned in the darkness to tell me of this magic sword that, only moments before, I had caught a glimpse of, not even knowing what it was. She told me of the old man who had stuck it there in the tree, and how many of her husband's friends had tried and failed to pull the magnificent weapon out of the trunk of that tree. As she drew nearer and nearer to me, she told me how my voice and my very face were the voice she heard and the face she saw as she sang in the forest and gazed into the woodland stream. As the beautiful night whispered to us in the moonlight, I found myself falling madly in love with this woman whom, I began to realize, I somehow already knew. And she, desperate to be saved from this awful existence with this dreadful husband, encouraged me to try my luck in freeing the sword from the tree.

With a massive effort, I pulled the sword free! Ecstatically, she gave me the name of Siegmund, and told me her name: Sieglinde! And now, with her husband drugged and asleep, and with this beautiful woman in my arms, I was overcome with love and passion—for my own sister. In the final moments of musical ecstasy, we consummated our love in the woods and then ran away together into the night.

What was this wonderful music that I had just heard? It seemed as if the words and the music were one; that I had been so totally engrossed in this lyric experience of awakening love and self-realization that I could have listened to this music over and over and never tired of it. It was so different from the Italian music that I had been getting acquainted with. There were no big arias for the most part, and those sections that seemed like arias flowed on in the story and held me waiting for every new thought and word to be expressed.

Had I been a tenor or a bass, I would have wanted to sing this music right away. But as a young baritone, I didn't feel an immediate desire to perform, but was overwhelmingly drawn to the power and beauty of it, nonetheless. Wagner was suddenly very real to me.

91

Thomas Stewart

Thomas Stewart (1928–2006; right, with J. K. Holman), the magnificent bass-baritone from Texas, burst into international prominence in Berlin in the late 1950s. He was soon tapped for roles at Bayreuth, eventually succeeding Hans Hotter there and elsewhere as the world's preeminent Wotan and Hans Sachs, roles he recorded with von Karajan and Kubelik, respectively.

After their singing careers, Tom and his wife, the acclaimed soprano Evelyn Lear, established themselves as highly regarded teachers. In 1999 they created the Evelyn Lear and Thomas Stewart Emerging Singers Program, a partnership with the Wagner Society of Washington, D.C., dedicated to the development of American singers with the potential for careers singing Wagner. Tom and Evelyn's continuing assistance to young singers reflects their commitment to the highest standards of good singing and dramatic comprehension.

Thomas Stewart died suddenly on September 24, 2006. Among the thousands of tributes, Marilyn Horne said: "He was vocal royalty—and one of the nicest human beings you could ever meet. We were privileged to have heard and known him."

During a performance of *Tannhäuser* at the Deutsche Oper in Berlin in 1965, I was singing Wolfram. In the first act, after the close of the Venusberg scene, the shepherd plays his tune and the arriving pilgrims intone the wonders of Rome. After that, there is a five-minute *banda*

section with the French horns, backstage, announcing the arrival of the hunting party.

I was in the wings, ready for my entrance and talking to the stage manager. We suddenly realized that the orchestral interlude had stopped and the conductor (Eugen Jochum) had made the downbeat for the horns to start their interlude backstage, but nothing happened. He gave the second downbeat, and again, silence. The horn players were in the *cantine*, having a beer, and had not been warned that their entrance was coming up!

I was watching the conductor on a backstage TV and saw him make a gesture of impatience, as he promptly launched into the orchestral music for the hunting scene. All the singers in the hunting scene were still in their dressing rooms. The missing horn section lasts at least five minutes, and they thought they had enough time to make it to the stage. As a result, there were no singers on stage to sing the opening lines of the hunting scene.

To bridge the gap of this embarrassing moment, I ran onstage, turned my back to the audience, made my voice as dark as possible, and sang the lines normally sung by the bass, Martti Talvela; then I switched to my fake tenor voice and sang two lines for one of the knights. By that time, my colleagues had arrived on stage, and the scene progressed normally.

At the end of the first act, Jochum came running up to Martti, thanking him profusely for preventing an embarrassing moment. Martti accepted his thanks, not knowing why (I later explained what had happened). I don't think Jochum, for as long as he lived, ever realized that Wolfram had saved the day!

I once gave a performance of *Siegfried* at the Vienna Staatsoper in 1969 with the well-known heldentenor, Hans Beirer, who tipped the scales at about 280 pounds. During the confrontation scene in Act III, the Wanderer tries to prevent Siegfried from climbing Brünnhilde's mountain. The stage directions called for me to hold the spear in front of him and for him to swing the sword Nothung, breaking the spear. Unfortunately, the spear did not break. It fell to the floor at such an angle that Herr Beirer walked over to it, jumped on it with all his might, and broke it to pieces.

This elicited huge laughs from the audience. Trying to maintain my dignity, I walked around the stage, gathering the broken pieces, and, trying to stifle my own laughter, exited the scene.

After the performances, some of my most ardent fans suggested that I keep the staging. After all the *Sturm und Drang*, a little levity was always welcome.

92

Jeffery Swann

Jeffrey Swann is one of America's finest concert pianists. Among other things, he recently completed a highly praised Beethoven sonata cycle in New York. He was recently named music director of the Cortina Festival.

Wagnerians know Swann as an unusually gifted lecturer and analyst who brings a double-barreled ability to convey the way Wagner's music and dramas work—at both the lectern and the piano.

I was fourteen years old and was going to boarding school in Dallas, Texas, where I lived in a house with a professor and eight other students. Because of my music, I had the very special privilege of being allowed to do homework in the professor's study in the evenings, while the professor listened to classical music on the radio. One evening while I was studying they announced on the classical station WRR-FM that they were going to play the Prelude and "Liebestod" from Wagner's *Tristan und Isolde.*

I specifically remember groaning inside because my image of Wagner—based entirely on ignorance—was that it was loud with heavy brass. But as soon as the Prelude started—right away, actually, with the very first pause—I was completely caught, and it was as if something extraordinary was being revealed to me. The power of the moment was not so much that I felt like I was discovering something new, on the outside, but that I was recognizing something that had been there all along, on the inside, and that it was becoming manifest. And I can truly say that at no other time in my life did listening to music make such a huge impression on me.

The result was that I was determined to get to know Wagner's music and works, so when I was visiting my grandmother the next weekend (she was a great opera lover and had Milton Cross's *Complete Stories of the Great Operas*) I read about *Tristan* and *The Ring* and was completely taken with the *Ring* story. Since I had no access to recordings of *The Ring* at that point, I borrowed the piano-vocal scores from the music library at Southern Methodist University, where I was studying as a special student, and I have to confess that I didn't return the books for five years. I started playing the scores the very next day and can honestly say I knew *Tristan* and most of *The Ring* by memory at the piano before I ever heard any of it with singers.

The postscript to this is that the next year I moved out of the boardinghouse and into the home of a couple with whom I stayed for my last three years of high school. They had a record player, and as I was going through their records, I discovered the Furtwängler recording of *Tristan*. At the first possible opportunity, I convinced them to go out of town and invited my best friend and fellow Wagner discoverer, Bobby Black, over to listen with me. So several months before my sixteenth birthday I listened to *Tristan* and had my first complete Wagner experience.

Roman Terleckyj

*Roman Terleckyj has long been one of the country's leading opera directors
and has won numerous awards for his work. He was for many years closely
associated with Gian Carlo Menotti and the Spoleto Festivals in Italy and
South Carolina. He was also head of production for the Washington Opera
and head of programming at the Kennedy Center for the Performing Arts in
Washington.*

My first try at staging Wagner was, to say the least, premature. With
only a few months to prepare, I was commandeered into remounting a
Parsifal that Gian Carlo Menotti had directed in Italy and then decided
to present at Charleston's Spoleto Festival. Too young to say no and too
full of myself to run as fast as I could from this demanding task (no
record of the original production remained), I pored over the score daily,
staring in ever mounting panic at what seemed to be unstageable acres
of words and music—including orchestral interludes that cried out for
scenic marvels.

Thoroughly daunted, I entered the rehearsal hall only to discover
that Wagner may well have been the best musical dramatist ever. Once
the staging began, a miraculous clock, seemingly built into the score,
suddenly took over and swept aside my fears. It was as if Wagner had
foreseen just how much music was needed to stage every element of the
work, from the smallest gesture to the most elaborate and drawn-out
ritual, with neither too few nor too many measures provided. What had
initially appeared to be vast and trackless stretches of score turned into
precise roadmaps drawn by the master. A fantastic lesson—but I still
should have waited!

Anthony Tommasini

Anthony Tommasini is the music critic of The New York Times. *The follow-ing review appeared in that newspaper on April 10, 2005. It begins with an eloquent Wagner Moment felt by Tommasini and many others—the remark-able and moving passage in the third scene of Act I of* Die Walküre *in which Sieglinde, perhaps the most sympathetic of all the* Ring *characters, tells her sad but noble story.*

    But the real value of the Tommasini piece is his pointed understanding of why this scene, along with others in Wagner, works so well: it is not about cosmic emotionalism or exaggerated sentiment, but rather Wagner's musical craftsmanship—technical, workmanlike, measure-by-measure—and above all, "the subtle yet ingenious harmonic manipulations of the motif."

    I can remember no other piece that lays out quite as well this crucial under-standing of Wagner's art.

Richard Wagner, Musical Mensch

There are moments in *Die Walküre*, Wagner's most humane opera, that never fail to dissolve me, even though I know they are coming. One occurs fairly early in the first act. During a terrible storm, a sad and fearful young woman trapped in an abusive marriage gives shelter to a ragged and sullen young man who has turned up at her door, injured and exhausted. They are strangers to each other, or so they think. Somehow the woman feels compelled to tell this outcast about her childhood—that a band of brutal warriors ransacked her home, murdered her mother, and forced her to marry a boorish clansman. On her miserable wedding night, her new husband's oafish friends came over to get drunk and ridicule her. But then, as the young woman tells her captivated visitor, a mysterious man in a gray cloak with a hat pulled down over one eye showed up uninvited. As the forlorn woman sings, the orchestra plays a quietly noble theme that sounds like a curiously subdued fanfare.

Those acquainted with Wagner's *Ring* cycle will recognize that theme as the motif of Valhalla, the castle of the gods. The music tells us that the man in the gray cloak was Wotan, the head god, and that the young woman and her exhausted visitor are Sieglinde and Siegmund, Wotan's twin children, who were brutally separated when little more than infants.

As the scene continues, Wagner turns the Valhalla motif into a harmonically luminous and deeply consoling extended passage. The transformed Valhalla motif signals to the audience (and in a subliminal way to Sieglinde) that she is not just a nobody, abused and laughed at by all: that she is a demigod, that her long-lost brother has arrived and that Wotan is looking out for her. Even if you don't recognize the motif, the music seems to sanctify Sieglinde as she tells her story.

Die Walküre returns to the Metropolitan Opera for two performances on April 19 and April 23. Valery Gergiev conducts. I suspect that once again I'll be overcome by this achingly sad exchange between Sieglinde and Siegmund (to be sung by Katarina Dalayman and Plácido Domingo), so full of mythical, spiritual, and psychological resonances.

But it is Wagner's music that gives this moment its impact: the subtle yet ingenious harmonic manipulations of the motif, the sonorous yet calmly subdued orchestration, Sieglinde's poignantly long-spun vocal line. I thought a lot about the specific character and qualities of Wagner's music as I slowly made my way through the latest biography of the composer, Richard *Wagner: The Last of the Titans* by the German author Joachim Kohler, first published four years ago in Germany and released late last year by Yale University Press in Stewart Spencer's English translation. Mr. Kohler focuses on Wagner's immense influence on German culture and history.

Striding through the seven hundred pages of this book is Wagner the aesthetician, the cultivator of myths, the Nietzschean superman, the megalomaniac, the shocking anti-Semite, the dramatic visionary. But Wagner the composer and musical craftsman make scant appearances.

Do not look here for musical analyses. Mr. Kohler has perceptive insights into Wagner's letters and essays. The discussions of his life and works are enriched by Mr. Kohler's Olympian knowledge of German history, philosophy, and politics. His analysis of *The Ring*, at nearly one hundred pages, takes the form of an engrossing retelling of the story, complete with fascinating comments drawn from his readings of the early drafts of Wagner's librettos.

Still, the questionable premise of this biography is that music in itself meant nothing to Wagner. "When he wrote it, it left no impression," Mr. Kohler writes. "Only when it drew its strength from the dramatic situations that were at the basis of his imagination did he succeed in creating anything that he could call his own. Music had to give expression to a world of living ideas."

I don't doubt that Wagner believed this; he certainly affirmed it in his essays. But I still don't buy it. Whether he knew it or not, Wagner was first and foremost a composer, inspired as much by harmony as by history, hooked as much by melody as by mythology. A lifelong student of the Beethoven symphonies and piano sonatas, he prepared detailed piano arrangements of the symphonies to earn money when he was young.

Mr. Kohler writes that what mattered to Wagner was not the feelings his art inspired but the ideas it communicated. "He expected nothing less from this message than that it would radically change the world, just as the Gospels had done," Mr. Kohler asserts.

Yes, this was Wagner's expectation, and yes, you could say that his art changed the world. But Wagner's manipulation of notes and rhythms played a big part in the process. Whatever convoluted philosophical notions filled his head in the fit of inspiration, his ear cut through the clutter when he sat down to compose.

To me, the real mystery of Wagner is that he became such a master craftsman despite his scattershot formal training. As a young man he studied a composition treatise on his own, took harmony lessons with a local musician in Dresden, and spent six intensive months working with the cantor of the Thomaskirche in Leipzig.

Mr. Kohler is at his best when he discusses the multiple layers of meaning in crucial scenes from *The Ring*. Toward the end of *Die Walküre*, for example, Wotan carries out the punishment he has decreed for his favorite Valkyrie daughter, Brünnhilde: she will be placed in a sleeping state on a mountain, surrounded by fire until such time as a mortal man will come to wake her and claim her. For all her wildness, as Mr. Kohler explains, Brünnhilde is not a creature of free will. She lives only to carry out her father's will. She is, as Fricka, Wotan's jealous wife, puts it, "the bride of his wishes." But not this time. When Wotan orders Brünnhilde not to side with his son, Siegmund, in the fight to death that he is about to have with Sieglinde's avenging husband, she is perplexed. How can Wotan do this? Siegmund is heroic; Siegmund is his child.

Though confused and uncertain, Brünnhilde tries to obey Wotan's order. But when she meets Siegmund and Sieglinde, she is moved beyond reason. She has never seen mortal love before. In deciding to aid Siegmund in the fight she divorces herself from Wotan's will and commits her first independent act. Wotan is furious. Having thrown her lot in with the mortals, Brünnhilde must become one, as her punishment. As she sinks into sleep, she loses her godhood.

But Mr. Kohler says nothing about the ingenious orchestral music with which Wagner conveys Brünnhilde's transformation. As a series of hushed, ethereal chords floats downward from on high, a parallel series of chords rises from below. The chords are mostly in the major mode, clear, diatonic and soothing. Yet as the bass line rises through an unconventional pattern of intervals (minor thirds and half-steps), touching all twelve tones of the chromatic scale on the way, the passage dislodges any sense of tonal stability.

The transfixing result is a strangely beautiful harmonic progression, at once calming and unhinged, that seems to descend and ascend at the same time. The music uncannily mimics what is happening to Brünnhilde as she sinks into a sleeping state losing her godliness but rising anew as a vulnerable mortal. When Mr. Kohler does discuss music, he says nothing specific enough to be valuable and sometimes loses all perspective. The "intimidating violence" of the storm music that opens *Die Walküre*, he writes, "had not hitherto been known in art." Oh, come on. I can think of passages from Bach Passions, Beethoven symphonies, and Schubert songs that convey intimidating violence as graphically as Wagner does.

Mr. Kohler thoroughly discusses Wagner's aesthetic treatises, like "The Artwork of the Future" and "Opera and Drama," essays that mix keen insights about the pragmatic needs of musical drama with lots of grandiose and muddled theories. There is a long and sober critical analysis of the repugnant essay "Jews in Music," in which Wagner argued that the honorable heritage of German music had been diluted by the slick and facile contributions of Jewish composers. But at some point, the only reaction you can have to Wagner's convoluted and hateful argument is to dismiss it as loony.

How did such sublime music come from such a warped man? Maybe art really does have the power to ferret out the best in us. One of the most awesome, wrenching, and profound performances of Beethoven's Ninth Symphony was made by Wilhelm Furtwängler, conducting the Berlin Philharmonic in 1942, when the Nazis were at the height of their power. Furtwängler's impassioned and volatile reading seems a tormented German musician's attempt to reveal Beethoven as an apocalyptic visionary. Still, it's eerie to hear an orchestra and chorus purged of Jews performing with palpable intensity a work that proclaims all men brothers.

Similarly, you can't tell me that the man who wrote *Die Walküre, Die Meistersinger,* and *Parsifal,* no matter how dreadful a character, did not somewhere in his being know compassion, tenderness, humility, parental devotion, and spiritual longing. But only by composing his astounding music could Wagner tap into those human feelings.

95

Arturo Toscanini

Perhaps the first conductor to rise to international superstardom, Toscanini (1867–1957) called Wagner the greatest composer of the nineteenth century. As Harvey Sachs has written,

Toscanini's love of the German composer's works took root during his Parma years, when the newness, forbiddenness, and unique beauty of the music had attracted him powerfully. His study of all of Wagner's scores and his experience conducting two of the earlier operas during the intervening years had greatly increased his admiration. Verdi he had imbibed with his mother's milk; but there is no doubt that Wagner was the great love of his youth. His re-evaluation and full recognition of the Italian master came after his wholehearted embracing of Wagner, surprisingly enough.

Tied in closely with this was his admiration of Wagner's writings—not the racial and chauvinistic ones, but the ideas on conducting and on the reorganization of theatrical practices. Wagner insisted that the conductor must seek not only technical excellence in working with the orchestra but must also use his imagination and intellect to try to grasp the outpouring of nervous energy, the difficult struggle toward expression, that lie behind the notes on the printed page (Toscanini, by Harvey Sachs [2002]).

Toscanini championed Wagner's operas and was instrumental in bringing them to an Italian audience. From the following letter Toscanini wrote to his wife from Turin in 1897, it is clear that he was also in favor of Wagnerian innovations such as darkening the theater during a performance, no matter the Italian reaction. This letter and the editor's note that follows it are taken from The Letters of Arturo Toscanini, *edited and translated by Harvey Sachs (2002).*

My dearest,

Yesterday, during the day, I had received a letter and newspapers from the greatest living evil eye caster. So how could I have avoided having some disgusting accident or other happen to me? You will have learned from the newspapers I've sent you what happened at the second *Tristan* performance—thus I have nothing to add to the report other than that I felt awful, really awful. I thought my head was going to split from one moment to the next, and yet I never for a moment stopped showing disrespect toward the audience. On the contrary, at the end of the second act they were calling for me to take a bow, but I refused, declaring openly in the middle of the stage (behind the closed curtain or front drop) that I was doing it on purpose, to show disrespect toward the audience. I won't tell you what I shouted at the journalists Bersezio and Berta in the presence of the owners of *La stampa* and *La gazzetta del popolo*, respectively, since all that pandemonium was their fault, a result of their asinine doings. Damn all the people who cast the evil eye!

The first performance of *Tristan* had gone excellently, although there was a bit of grumbling from some members of the public because AT had insisted on keeping the auditorium dark during the performance: in those days, audiences were accustomed to having half-light in the auditorium so that they could walk around, chat, eat, observe one another, flirt, play cards, and follow libretti while "listening" to an opera. The next day's newspapers gave exaggerated reports of the grumbling, thus provoking a verbal battle at the second performance. AT had to stop conducting, and when the management turned the lights on he lost his temper and smashed the light on his music stand. The remainder of the performance took place in half-light, but AT was so angry that he conducted the rest of the opera sitting in his chair, his right hand resting on his knee, and barely moved his baton. Poor Polo virtually had to lead the orchestra, while the prompter tried to assist the singers. Like most theater people, AT was superstitious, and he was especially wary of people who were said to have the evil eye.

96

Astrid Varnay

Astrid Varnay (1918–2006) was born in Stockholm. Both her parents were Hungarian, and were opera singers at the Royal Swedish Opera. She used to say that her mother, singing in Un ballo in maschera, *once used a drawer in a dressing room as a makeshift crib, and her babysitter that night—was Kirsten Flagstad!*

The family ultimately moved to New York, where Varnay was hired to sing at the Met. One morning in December 1941, she came to the Met to rehearse for her first stage performance, as Elsa in Lohengrin, *which was to take place the next month. The following describes a unique Wagner Moment and is taken from her autobiography* 55 Years in Five Acts *(2000), written with Donald Arthur.*

As I stepped into the room, [Erich Leinsdorf] greeted me rather cryptically with the question: "What are we rehearsing today?" At first, I didn't catch on that Leinsdorf might have been trying to tell me something, and simply said, "I suppose we'll continue working on Elsa." The conductor replied that he wanted to check through the role of Sieglinde in *Die Walküre*. There was no need, Leinsdorf told me, to sing out. I was welcome to "mark"—that is to say, sing half-voice or take the top notes an octave lower—something all professional singers do to spare their voices and keep them in trim for the big rehearsals and the performances. I still wasn't quite sure why he didn't want to hear the Sieglinde full voice, with no performances scheduled for me until after the New Year, but he was the boss.

After I had warbled through Sieglinde from start to finish, the maestro nonchalantly told me to report to the make-up and costume department. Then the penny dropped. I later discovered that Mme. Lotte Lehmann had a cold, which had forced her to cancel the Saturday matinee. Somebody else would have to take over for her.

Editor's note: The next day the twenty-three-year-old Varnay triumphed in front of "friends from my standing room days." However, the favorable reviews were buried in other news—the attack on Pearl Harbor! The story does not end here, though, because six days later, Helen Traubel canceled her Die Walküre *Brünnhilde, and Varnay took that role as well, again to triumphant reviews. She finally "managed to make my 'official' debut, singing* Elsa in Lohengrin *the first month of the New Year, and my career was off and running (at $75 a week!)."*

In the past couple of years we have lost Astrid Varnay, Brigit Nilsson, and Elisabeth Schwarzkopf. We can only hope to hear their like again.

97

Paul Verlaine

Paul Verlaine (1844–1896) remains one of France's most notorious and influential poets. In both his poetry and personal life he, like Baudelaire and Mallarmé, will always be associated with the Symbolists and the Decadents. In 1884 he coined the term "poètes maudits," a name taken from a series of essays praising other "outcast" poets. His tempestuous life included wealth, marriage, affairs with Arthur Rimbaud and young boys, poverty, professional recognition, prison, prostitutes, public hospitals, Catholicism, and alcoholism, among other things.

His poems often deal with the possibility of redemption through love. But he is celebrated more for style than substance, especially for his groundbreaking mastery of the French language for its rhythm and musicality.

Verlaine's poem "Parsifal" appeared in *Le revue wagnérienne* (see Wagner Moment 80) in 1886. The final line of this poem is quoted in "The Waste Land" (see Wagner Moments 28 and 53).

Parsifal a vaincu les Filles, leur gentil
Babil et al luxure amusante—et sa pente
Vers la Chair de garçon vierge que cela tente
D'aimer les seins légers et ce gentil babil;

Il vaincu la Femme belle, au coeur subtil,
Étalant ses bras frais et sa gorge excitante;
Il a vaincu l'Enfer et rentre sous sa tente
Avec un lourd trophée à son bras puéril,

Avec la lance qui perça le Flanc suprême!
Il a guéri le roi, le voici roi lui-même,
Et prêtre du très saint Trésor essentiel.

En robe d'or il adore, gloire et symbole,
Le vase pur où resplendit le Sang réel.
—Et, ô ces voix d'enfants chantant dans la coupole!

Parsifal has overcome the gently babbling daughters
Who'd distract him to desire; despite fleshly delight
That might lure the virgin youth, the temptation
To love their swelling breasts and gentle babble;

He has vanquished fair Womankind, of subtle heart,
Her tender arms outstretched and her throat pale;
From harrowing Hell, he now returns triumphant,
Bearing a heavy trophy in his boyish hands,

With the spear that pierced the Savior's side!
He who healed the King shall be himself enthroned,
As priest-king and guardian of the sacred treasure.

In golden robe he worships that sign of grace,
The pure vessel in which shines the Holy Blood.
—And, o those children's voices singing in the dome!

Shirley Verrett

I suspect that anyone who ever heard Shirley Verrett will carry a permanent impression of that radiant sound and stunning versatility. Both "The Song of the Veil" (for sheer technical virtuosity) and "O don fatale" (for astounding dramatic lyricism), in the Giulini recording of Don Carlo, *are among my most vivid Verdi Moments.*

Sustained by her devout religious upbringing, yet overcoming its strictures to reach the operatic stage, Verrett has repeatedly given back, by her active support for civil rights, the performing arts, young singers, and other causes.

The following excerpt is taken from her autobiography, I Never Walked Alone. *Wagnerians can only wonder at what might have happened had the* London Tristan *not been canceled.*

I returned to London for my first Brangäne opposite Birgit Nilsson in *Tristan und Isolde* at Covent Garden that May, but Birgit became ill and had to withdraw from the performance. Instead of hiring another singer, the management decided to cancel the production.

I remember the process of working on that role. My voice seemed to acquire a weight and coloration unusual for me. It actually scared me a bit. I think my voice took on more heft because of the language and the music of Wagner. I never performed that role anywhere, although I would have liked to. I have often thought about the heft I felt coming into my voice and wondered where it would have taken me.

Frederica von Stade

Frederica von Stade has long been a treasure of American music, and one of opera's most beloved figures. Von Stade started at the top, hired by Sir Rudolph Bing to sing at the Met during the Metropolitan Opera auditions. She created a sensation in 1970 singing Susanna in The Marriage of Figaro. *In recent years, the Met has created new productions of* The Merry Widow *and* Pelléas et Mélisande *for her. She has sung leading roles in every major opera house in the world.*

Von Stade's orchestral and recital successes are equally broad and include music of every period from the baroque to the present. She is especially regarded as an interpreter of the vast French repertoire.

In 1998 Richard Danielpour composed Elegies for her, scored for orchestra, mezzo-soprano, and baritone and based on letters her father wrote to her mother shortly before his death in World War II, two months before her own birth.

Von Stade, whom friends and fans call Flicka, has made over seventy recordings with every major recording label, in the process winning countless awards.

Wagnerians can only regret that she is no longer appearing as a Flower Maiden.

I have a most modest connection to Wagner. I once sang one of the *Blumenmädchen* about thirty-five years ago at the Metropolitan Opera. I was new to opera, hadn't heard of Mozart (if you can believe it) much less Wagner. So I have memories mainly of a certain level of difficulty as to which line to sing (there were six of us) and finding one's way around the stage, up and down ramps with hats on that were quite large and that had annoying little balls on the end of the "petals" that used to get caught on anything, even another *Blumenmädchen* as we ran up and down these quite dangerous ramps singing our bluming hearts out. It was a lot of fun, sometimes a little silly, and part of the rich tapestry of *opera*.

Stephen Wadsworth

Stephen Wadsworth has established a reputation as one of the world's leading stage and opera directors. His work has covered the classic repertoires in both drama and opera the world over. Among his major triumphs is the acclaimed Ring *in Seattle (2001 and 2005), where he has also directed* The Flying Dutchman *and* Lohengrin.

Wadsworth is an award-winning translator, having adapted the works of Handel, Monteverdi, Mozart, Molière, and Marivaux. His translation and direction of Molière's Don Juan *in Washington in 2006 was a major success. He is also a librettist, having written* A Quiet Place *for Leonard Bernstein in 1983.*

I grew up in a very un-Wagnerian home; my grandfather had famously slept through *Siegfried* and missed the dragon, and my parents seemed unable or unwilling to metabolize Wagner, focusing instead on Handel, Bach, and Mozart, with an occasional *Butterfly* or *Trovatore*, and floods of tears for the end of *Rosenkavalier*.

I realized it was up to me to try to fathom Wagner, so I sat down with a George London recording of "Die Frist ist um" from *Fliegende Holländer*, and the door opened on that hypnotic, disturbing world where torments of the heart and mind are articulated with such forbidding subtlety. *Walküre* came next, with its moral challenges—intriguing, sweeping, huge.

When I was a senior in high school I played Thomas Becket in T. S. Eliot's *Murder in the Cathedral*, a play detailing Becket's inner debate about martyrdom and pondering his motives. I found I needed a time of concentrated meditation before a rehearsal or performance—there was such a distance between my daily life and the journey Becket had to take—and what I did was lie down and play the final scene of *Walküre*, from Wotan's entrance to the end. In a rehearsal of the scene in which Becket is tempted, essentially by voices in his head, a long scene of kneeling, listening, and trying to decide, I heard Brünnhilde's voice in Thomas Becket's head, singing "Der diese Liebe mir ins Herz gehaucht" (One man's love breathed this into my heart).

Subsequently Thomas and I heard it in our shared head every time we lived through that scene together.

I know that the constant forward movement of the music was a great help to me as a young actor in learning how to let thought flow forward, but there was another reason this music came into play. It spoke to Becket's temptation. Wotan and Brünnhilde's wrangling over the issue of volition, over how and why to act, and over what was truly the right thing to do had already led me into Becket's waters, and it loomed up in my heart as I came to play that scene, a vivid emotional memory for a young actor facing a scene of great moral complexity and looking for common ground.

That's when I realized that Wagner was in my system, when I first felt grateful to him, personally, for helping me.

101

Alan Wagner

Alan Wagner's voice is familiar to opera lovers from his many appearances on the Metropolitan Opera broadcast intermissions over the years. In addition, he lectures frequently. He has been an adjunct professor at Syracuse and New York Universities.

Alan Wagner was the host and commentator for six New York City Opera radio broadcast seasons, and for ten years before that produced and hosted a weekly radio program called Living Opera. *A frequent contributor of articles and reviews to the Metropolitan Opera,* Playbill, *and* Opera News, *he has also appeared in such diverse publications as the* New York City Opera Souvenir Book, High Fidelity, Musical America, Stage Bill, *and* Reader's Digest. *His book* Prima Donnas and Other Wild Beasts *is now undergoing revision, expansion, and updating for a new edition.*

In his day job, Alan Wagner is a television programmer, producer, and consultant to major broadcast and cable companies. He spent over two decades in a senior creative role at the CBS Television Network during the so-called Tiffany years, where he developed programs such as All in the Family, M*A*S*H, Maude, Kojak, The Bob Newhart Show, The Waltons, *and* The Mary Tyler Moore Show. *He was also responsible for many cultural broadcasts from the Balanchine/Stravinsky "The Flood" and "The Return of Vladimir Horowitz" to "Sills and Burnett at the Met."*

Alan Wagner was the first president and CEO of the Disney Channel, after which he formed Boardwalk Entertainment, an independent film and television production company he now owns with his wife and daughters.

The works of Richard Wagner are so central to me that, when asked to describe my singular Wagner Moment, a host of possibilities sprang to mind—my first complete *Ring*; the great choral outbreak in Act III of *Die Meistersinger*; maybe my initial immersion—live—into the sound world of *Parsifal*, certainly a transformative experience.

But one memory kept intruding into all these—a much more modest occasion, but in the end, the one that altered my life and turned me into a Wagnerian forever, and unwittingly.

I was very young, living near a beach in Brooklyn, spending all my afternoons outside playing with friends, even on Saturdays, when the rest of my family gathered around our ancient radio to listen to Met opera broadcasts. For some reason, on one of these afternoons I returned to our apartment briefly—and came screeching to a halt. I heard music in that room that stunned me, immobilized me. I was literally transfixed.

It lasted only a few moments: the final scene of an April 3, 1937, broadcast of *Das Rheingold*. I did not breathe until after the gods had all entered Valhalla to that deceptively triumphant music. Only later did I know I was hearing Bodansky conducting Schorr and Branzell with René Maison as Loge. That day I didn't care.

The enchantment had already worked even before I received a bare-bones précis of the story from my father, but then I knew this was about curses and giants and gods who conjured up and walked across a Rainbow Bridge. All raw meat for a very young kid, and I became voracious, listening to every 78-rpm record of *Ring* music the Brooklyn Public Library owned, reading every book I could lay hands on. I was hooked, and time has only deepened the magic since that miraculous afternoon almost three-quarters of a century ago.

102

Richard Wagner

The year 1861, like so many years in Wagner's life (1813–1883), was marked by struggle and frustration. After the Tannhäuser *scandal in Paris, he returned to Vienna to face insurmountable obstacles to a* Tristan *staging, reproaches from distant Minna on their silver wedding anniversary, and the usual problems of inadequate revenues, increasing living expenses, and continuing dependence upon the hospitality of others: "And so I had to confess that my situation was pretty miserable."*

Wagner's words here are from the definitive translation of his autobiography, Mein Leben, *by Andrew Gray. Andrew, a civil servant in the U.S. government, was for many years, until his recent death, among the most knowing of Wagner scholars and a magnificent champion and unapologetic defender of Wagner.*

As with so many Wagner episodes, it makes little difference in the overall scheme of things whether there is any literal truth to the following story. Wagner had probably made his decision to embark on Die Meistersinger *a couple of weeks before leaving Vienna, and he saw the* Assumption *at the Academy of Art, not the Palace of the Doges. The picture now hangs over the central altar of the Chiesa del Frari, the big Venetian church that houses Canova's tomb.*

Wagner's Titian Moment

In a casual conversation with the Wesendoncks I had made no secret how things stood; apparently with the objective of cheering me up, they invited me to meet them in Venice, where they were just about to go on a pleasure trip. Heaven knows what I had in mind when I set off one gray November day to go by rail to Trieste, and from there with a steamboat, which made me sick, to reach Venice and proceed to my little room in the Hotel Danieli. My friends, whom I found in flourishing circumstances, were reveling in enjoyment of the paintings and seemed to have it in mind to dispel my depression by sharing these delights. They seemed disinclined to realize what my position was in Vienna, and indeed, after the failure of the Paris venture that had been attended by so many glorious hopes, I increasingly found that most of my friends had tacitly abandoned hopes for my future success. Wesendonck, who was always armed with a huge opera glass, ready to inspect works of art, managed to induce me only once to visit the Palace of the Doges, a building which I had known only from the outside on my former visit to Venice. I have to admit that despite all my apathy Titian's *Assumption of the Virgin* in the great hall of the Doges made a most exalting impression upon me, so that by this inspiration I found my old creative powers awakening within me with almost their original primordial power.

I decided to write *Die Meistersinger.*

103

John Ward

John Ward (left, with Carlo Rizzi, WNO's music director) is the London-based development advisor to the Welsh National Opera. He joined the Bank of England after graduating from university but gave up full-time banking to establish a trade union to represent bank staff. After running the union for several years, he became general secretary of the First Division Association, the union for top civil servants, negotiating with Prime Minister Margaret Thatcher, among others. In 1988 he was appointed development director at Opera North in Leeds and subsequently held similar posts with the West Yorkshire Playhouse and English National Opera.

My Wagner Moment came towards the beginning of Act II of *Tristan und Isolde* at about 6:35 p.m. on Saturday, August 8, 1959, at Bayreuth. I was a teenager attending my third-ever opera. (The previous two had been *Lohengrin* and *Parsifal*, a few nights before—an interesting way to begin one's operagoing! Interesting, too, that in those days one could simply write to the Bayreuth box office from school and they sent you tickets!)

Birgit Nilsson was already in full flood by the time she reached the passage beginning "Dein Werk? O tor'ge Magd" (Your deed? O, foolish maid). As the tempo broadens at the climactic "es werde Nacht, dass hell sie dorten leuchte" ([the goddess of love desires] night to come, that she may brightly shine there), and more precisely at the notes on "hell" I felt something hit me in the pit of the stomach in a way that catapulted the rest of my body forward, leaving my stomach far behind and the whole of me elated, breathless, and tingling through most of the ensuing love duet.

I have twice subsequently had a similar experience. First at a football match when the Chelsea center forward, Tony Hateley, who was reputed to head a ball harder than he kicked it, met a ferocious cross from the winger, Bobby Tambling, and the ball flew from his head into the net before the goalkeeper could move and almost faster than we could see. The other time I was sprawled across the back seat of a friend's Aston Martin—the roof was too low for me to sit—while it was stationary at a traffic light. The light turned green, Peter stamped on the accelerator, and the car flew forward, leaving me breathless and my stomach pinned to my seat, as Wagner and Nilsson had done before.

Thus did my Wagner Moment show me, in addition to its emotional, intellectual, and spiritual qualities, the sheer physical impact of his music!

104

Michael Wiedman

"Dr. Mike" is one of the United States' preeminent eye surgeons. He practices and teaches at the Harvard Medical School and Massachusetts Eye Infirmary. He is both an accomplished mountain climber and the world's leading authority on high-altitude sickness, having been the medical officer on numerous major expeditions, including five to Mount Everest.

Wiedman annually travels to the world's most impoverished communities to perform eye surgeries and provide other medical services pro bono.

The setting in the Swiss Alps was veritably Valhalla. Between the Matterhorn and Monte Rosa in roseate glow, "Morgenlich leuchtend in rosigen Schein," we hiked in joyous company. Echoing through the valley, the crag martin twittered. A deer skittered. The ibex was aloft.

Below, rising *träumerisch* along the steep trail, a Wagner aria drifted across the crags, steadily increasing in fervor. *Die Meistersinger* was loosed upon the hills. The unknown, tenuous tenor as Walther, too, delivered his song.

> Twice-blessed day,
> that dawned upon a poet's dream!
> The paradise I longed to know
> in Heaven's new transfigured gleam
> shining it lay . . .

Unknown to the lyrical singer, I tripped swiftly down the gorge to proffer bravos. Bursting upon him below, I encountered a pair of swinging shoulders and striving legs in cadence with the tempo. The fellow hiker, in *alpenschuwerk* and *alpenstock*, was singing in secret reverie.

During a rest in his song, in my Wagner Moment, I aired a thankful Pilgrim's return, mine,

> My heart grows light
> as I see once more
> My pilgrim's staff
> I lay to rest. . . .

Thus motivated, I was spontaneously accompanied by that very mountaineer in convivial duet. Enclasped in lyrical brotherhood, an epiphany, the Wagner Moment crescendoed with

> For ever songs of praise
> I'll sing Alleluia for evermore!

105

Simon Williams

Simon Williams is chairman of the drama department at the University of California, Santa Barbara. He is a frequent guest lecturer on drama and music, including at the Bayreuth Festival. His most recent book is Wagner and the Romantic Hero.

As a teacher of drama, I have spent years telling my students that our enjoyment of a work of theater does not necessarily depend solely upon our own feelings or moods, but upon those of other people in the audience. For most of those years, however, I am not quite sure I fully believed that myself. However, the truth of this was brought home to me very strikingly during a performance of *Parsifal* at Bayreuth.

The morning prior to the performance I had delivered a long lecture on *Parsifal* in which I had dwelt in particular upon the peculiar way in which drama and ritual are intertwined in Wagner's last work, so that ultimately *Parsifal* can be interpreted as being a work about ritual. To have its full impact, I had argued, the audience must possess faith in the values that are being represented on stage, faith akin to that which a congregation feels in a church or other house of worship.

That evening's performance did not, however, seem as if it would come close to fulfilling the ritualistic potential of the music drama, at least as far as I was concerned. For some reason, I was in a rotten mood and felt very much out of sorts; the opening act that I normally find so moving had left me completely cold, and I mooched out of the Festspielhaus wondering whether I might not forgo the next two acts, something I have done only two or three times in a very long operagoing career, and never for Wagner.

As I was pondering what to do, a Canadian lady who had attended my talk in the morning came up to me and asked me what I thought. I was about to deliver a rather sour judgment on the performance when she forestalled me by looking up to the sky and saying in a rapt voice, "This is the most wonderful experience of my life."

Quite clearly she had been so transformed by what she had seen that it would have been churlish and unforgivable for me to say anything that would take her out of her ecstasy. So I mustered as much enthusiasm as I could, which turned out to be more than I might have expected, and agreed with her that this truly was a remarkable experience, something that I might treasure for a lifetime. I did, however, feel somewhat hypo-critical in doing so.

I stayed, however, perhaps out of a feeling of guilt that if someone could be as deeply moved as this lady had been, I must be missing out on something. I returned to the Festspielhaus with my bad mood put on hold, at least temporarily. And I am glad I did. I saw and heard the last two acts with her ears and eyes, not with my own, and it was transforma-tive. Ever since, I have been able to find ever greater beauties in Wagner's luminous score every time I hear it. It was this lady who showed me the way to understand the greatness of his last work.

106

Virginia Woolf

Early success, subsequent neglect, and feminist resurrection has characterized the critical standing of Virginia Woolf (1882–1941). Today her reputation as one of the foremost writers of the twentieth century seems secure. By some, she is judged (unlike Wagner) as lacking in "universality and depth, without the power to communicate anything of emotional or ethical relevance to the disillusioned common reader, weary of the 1920s aesthetes." But by others she is credited (like Wagner) for probing "the underlying psychological as well as emotional motives of characters." In the words of E. M. Forster, she pushed the English language "a little further against the dark."

Like Thomas Mann and Friedrich Nietzsche, Woolf fully engaged Wagner's operas, and sometimes she changed her mind about them.

The following excerpt is taken from Virginia Woolf *(1995) by James King (a student, forty years ago, of Father Owen Lee at the University of Toronto).*

Since her visits to lush, sun-filled Italy with the Bells had not been a success, she chose to go to Bayreuth and later to Dresden with Adrian and Saxon [Sydney-Turner] in August 1909. At this time Virginia was open to Wagnerian splendor, particularly the way in which sexual and religious experiences are fused together—an accomplishment she felt was difficult to describe: "Somehow Wagner has conveyed the desire of the Knights for the Grail in such a way that the intense emotion of human beings is combined with the earthly nature of the things they seek."

Her observations continue with an even more resplendent compliment: "Like Shakespeare, Wagner seems to have attained in the end to such a mastery of technique he could float and soar in regions where in the beginning he could scarcely breathe; the stubborn matter of his art dissolves in his fingers, and he shapes it as he chooses."

In August 1909, Woolf wrote a long article for *The Times*, "Impressions at Bayreuth," which concludes as follows:

Here at Bayreuth, where the music fades into the open air, and we wander with *Parsifal* in our heads through empty streets at night, where the gardens of the Hermitage glow with flowers like those other magic blossoms, and sound melts into colour, and colour calls out for words, where, in short, we are lifted out of the ordinary world and allowed merely to breathe and see—it is here that we realize how thin are the walls between one emotion and another; and how fused our impressions are with elements which we may not attempt to separate.

107

Francesca Zambello

Francesca Zambello is an internationally esteemed director of opera and theater. Since her debut with a production of Fidelio *at Houston, she has directed more than 160 operas around the world. In 2006 she directed* Das Rheingold, *initiating the first-ever* Ring *cycle at the Washington National Opera.*

Heinz Fricke, who recently celebrated his sixtieth year as conductor, has been the musical director and principal conductor at the WNO since 1993. He is considered one of his generation's leading conductors of Mozart, Beethoven—and Wagner.

The former home of the Royal Danish Opera was the eight-hundred-seat King's Theater in Copenhagen, which dates from the eighteenth century. The first works of Wagner I ever staged were for this ensemble company—*Tannhäuser* in 1992 and then *Meistersinger* in 1994. While there I first met up with this crotchety German conductor who I thought would drive me crazy with his adherence to traditions. As it turned out, Heinz Fricke is one of the greatest collaborators I could ever have dreamed of. Not only has he taught me so much about Wagner, but even more, we have shared a true collaboration between conductor and director.

I will never forget the emotion-packed opening night of *Meistersinger* when we had two hundred cast members onstage, as well as all the backstage crew, plus a hundred musicians in the pit—that meant there were half as many people working on the show as there were in the audience. With the arrival of the Masters for the Festweise we felt as though we were all experiencing their celebration as one complete and united artistic community. I had the trumpets enter from the auditorium (because they would never have fit on the stage), so I brought them into the aisles, suggesting that the Festweise was our collective journey. It was for me a joyous, life-affirming moment and a career highlight.

The combination of this music with all of the stage joining together for a communal emotion with the audience makes for one of those rushes live theater can bring when you feel your hair stand up and tears come to your eyes, reaffirming that these times only come once every few years and are worth the wait.

Epilogue

Authors and editors often provide bona fides at the beginning of their work. In addition, I have often been asked about my own Wagner Moments. On some reflection, I thought it prudent to kill both of these birds with a single stone, and for reasons which will be obvious, here at the end. Regretfully, the following story is quite true.

A few years ago Mrs. Holman and I were enjoying a hiking trip in the Lake District of northern England. Upon checking out of our hotel, I noticed a magnificent bust of Wagner in the foyer. It was fashioned, as I recall it, out of the most attractive rosewood, and the features of the great man—the high forehead and hawklike nose—were masterfully rendered.

Returning home, I wrote to the proprietor of the hotel, telling him what a splendid place it was, how much we had enjoyed our stay, and wondering if he would consider selling the Wagner bust.

I received a courteous reply in due course, in which I was informed how much our patronage of the hotel had been appreciated, hoping that we would return someday, and informing me that, sadly, the bust to which I had referred was not Wagner, but "our great Scottish novelist, Sir Walter Scott."

In June 1955 Ernest Newman, England's most acclaimed music critic for fifty years and the most significant Wagner scholar of the first half of the century (see Wagner Moment 70), lay dying, suffering from a wide variety of crippling and painful ailments.

The following account of his final Wagner Moment is taken from Ernest Newman: A Memoir, *published by his wife, Vera, in 1964.*

He told me he would like to hear *Parsifal*. I asked him which particular part he wanted me to play, and I was surprised when he said he wanted to hear all of it. I said I thought it would be too tiring for him, but he

said, on the contrary, it would do him good. He would not even let me
pause between the acts and we played through the whole of the long
opera without a break except for the time necessary to turn the records
over. I did not take my eyes from his face all the time the records were
playing, looking for any signs of fatigue; but I was amazed and fascinated
by his complete concentration on the music. I always knew when he was
absorbed in something, because he had a habit of moving his eyes as if
he were reading a score. He made one remark during the performance:
"That sounds like Ludwig Weber at his very best," he said, after one of
Gurnemanz's long solos. I reminded him that this was the recording
of the Bayreuth performance we had heard, and it *was* Weber at his
very best.

He was moved, as always, by the "Good Friday Music," and also
by the scene of the Recognition of the Holy Spear by Gurnemanz in
the first scene of the last act. When it was finished he said to me: "You
know, I have some new ideas about this, I think I shall have to do a little
book on it."

So, you see, even at the end, as long as we are alive, there is the always the
possibility of Wagner Moments.

Sources and Permissions

Every effort has been made to seek out and obtain permissions from the copyright holders of the pieces and illustrations included in this book. Text selections, photographs, and other artwork are reproduced courtesy of the respective authors and of the following:

Woodcuts courtesy of Melissa Merkling.

Peter Allen. Photograph courtesy of the Metropolitan Opera Archives.

Margaret Atwood. Photograph by George Whiteside.

W. H. Auden. From *Auden* by Richard Davenport-Hines (New York: Pantheon, 1995). Photograph by Antony Di Gesu, courtesy of San Diego Historical Society.

Joe Banno. Photograph by Clare Newman-Williams.

Daniel Barenboim. From *Parallels and Paradoxes* by Daniel Barenboim and Edward W. Said (London: Bloomsbury, 2002). Photograph © 1999 Richard Haughton, Warner Classics.

Charles Baudelaire. From *Baudelaire* by Joanna Richardson (New York: St. Martin's Press, 1994). Photograph by Etienne Carjat.

Lord Berners. From *A Distant Prospect* by Lord Berners (New York: Turtle Point Press/Helen Marx Books, 1998).

Günter Blobel. Photograph © The Nobel Foundation.

Richard Bradshaw. Photograph courtesy of Canadian Opera Company.

Willa Cather. From "A Wagner Matinee," *Great Short Works by Willa Cather* by Willa Cather (New York: Harper Perennial, 1993). Photograph courtesy of Willa Cather Pioneer Memorial Collection, Nebraska State Historical Society.

Paul Cézanne. From *Cézanne* by Henri Loyrette (London: Tate Gallery, 1996). *Girl at the Piano* by Paul Cézanne © The State Hermitage Museum, St. Petersburg.

Marcia Davenport. From *Of Lena Geyer* by Marcia Davenport (New York: Charles Scribner's Sons, 1936).

Jonathan Dean. Photograph by Rozarii Lynch.

Achille-Claude Debussy. From *Debussy: His Life and Mind* by Edward Lockspeiser (Cambridge: Cambridge University Press, 1965). Photograph by Félix Nadar, courtesy of the Piano Society. Photograph © David Seymour/Magnum Photos.

John Louis DiGaetani. Photograph courtesy of Hofstra University.

Plácido Domingo. Photograph by Winnie Klotz, Metropolitan Opera.

Les Dreyer. Letter to the Editor by Les Dreyer, *New York Times,* May 1, 2005.

T. S. Eliot. From *Wagner: The Terrible Man and His Truthful Art* by M. Owen Lee (Toronto: University of Toronto Press, 1999). Photograph © The Nobel Foundation.

Martin Feinstein. Photograph courtesy of Marcia Feinstein.

Sherman Finger. Photograph by Martha Finger, courtesy of the University of Southern California.

Benjamin Foster. Photograph by Michael Marsland, Yale University, Office of Public Affairs.

Peter Gelb. Photograph by Dario Acosta, courtesy of the Metropolitan Opera Archives.

Pamela Jones Harbour. Photograph courtesy of the Federal Trade Commission.

Daniel Herwitz. Photograph courtesy of Doretha Coval.

Adams Holman. Photograph by Hilary Shaw.

Marilyn Horne. Photograph courtesy of the Marilyn Horne Foundation.

Hans Hotter. From *Hans Hotter: Memoirs* by Hans Hotter, translated and edited by Donald Arthur (Lebanon, NH: Northeastern University Press, 2006).

Linda and Michael Hutcheon. Photograph by John Reeves.

Henry James. From *Henry James: A Life* by Leon Edel (New York: Harper and Row, 1985). Photograph by Alice Baughton, courtesy of Penn State University Photo Archives.

Speight Jenkins. Photograph courtesy of Seattle Opera.

James Joyce. From *James Joyce: A Portrait of the Artist* by Stan Gébler Davies (New York: Stein and Day, 1975).

Wassily Kandinsky. From *Kandinsky: Compositions* by Magdalena Dabrowski (New York: The Museum of Modern Art, 1995).

Alexandra Kauka. Photograph by Kevin Lamb.

Winnie Klotz. Photograph by Winnie Klotz.

Evelyn Lear. Photograph courtesy of The Wagner Society of Washington, D.C.

M. Owen Lee. Photograph by Iain Scott.

Oscar Levant. From *The Unimportance of Being Oscar* by Oscar Levant (New York: Putnam, 1968).

Claude Lévi-Strauss. From *Conversations with Claude Lévi-Strauss* by Claude Lévi-Strauss and Didier Eribon (Chicago: University of Chicago Press, 1991).

Bernard Levin. From *"Parsifal"* by Bernard Levin, *Times (London)*, February 18, 1988.

Michael Levine. Photograph courtesy of Canadian Opera Company.

C. S. Lewis. From *Surprised by Joy: The Shape of My Early Life* by C. S. Lewis (New York: HarperCollins, 1998). Copyright © 1956 by C. S. Lewis and renewed 1984 by Arthur Owen Barfield. Reprinted by permission of Harcourt, Inc. Photograph courtesy of the C. S. Lewis Foundation.

Saul Lilienstein. Photograph by Diana Holman.

George and Nora London. From *Aria for George* by Nora London (New York: Dutton, 1987).

Laura Maioglio. From "De Sabata's Outstanding New York Philharmonic Wagner Concert" by Dan Davis, CD program note in *Wagner: Estratti Operistic*, 2001.

Thomas Mann. From *The Thomas Mann Reader* by Thomas Mann, translated and edited by Joseph Warner Angell (New York: Alfred A. Knopf, 1950). Photograph © The Nobel Foundation.

Peter Mark. Photograph courtesy of Virginia Opera.

Alisdair Neale. Photograph by R. J. Muna.

Ernest Newman. From *Ernest Newman: A Memoir* by Vera Newman (New York: Alfred A. Knopf, 1964).

Friedrich Nietzsche. From *Nietzsche* by Curtis Cates (New York: Overlook Press, 2002). Photograph by F. Hartmann.

Ignacy Jan Paderewski. Photograph courtesy of Project Gutenberg Archives.

Tim Page. Photograph by Jim Balmer.

Jan Peerce. From *Bluebeard of Happiness: The Memoirs of Jan Peerce* by Jan Peerce with Alan Levy (New York: HarperCollins, 1976).

Marcel Proust. From *Marcel Proust: Selected Letters, 1880–1903*, by Marcel Proust, edited by Philip Kolb, translated by Ralph Manheim (New York: Doubleday, 1983) and *Marcel Proust: Selected Letters, 1918–1921*, by Marcel Proust, edited by Philip Kolb, translated by Joanna Kilmartin (London: HarperCollins, 2000).

Pierre-Auguste Renoir. From *Renoir: The Man, the Painter, and His World* by Lawrence Hanson (New York: Dodd, Mead, 1968) and *Renoir, My Father* by Jean Renoir, translated by Randolph and Dorothy Weaver (New York: New York Review Books, 2001), courtesy of the William Morris Agency. Portrait of Richard Wagner by Pierre-Auguste Renoir, courtesy of Musée d'Orsay.

La Revue Wagnérienne. *"A French Connection" by Bet Briggs, www.bikwil. com.*

John Singer Sargent and Judith Gautier. From *Sargent* by Richard Ormond (London: Tate Gallery, 1998). *A Gust of Wind* by John Singer Sargent, courtesy of The Athenaeum.

Christina Scheppelmann. Photograph courtesy of Washington National Opera.

Iain Scott. Photograph by Barbara Scott.

Beverly Sills. Photograph courtesy of Vincent & Farrell Associates.

Georg Solti. From *Memoirs* by Sir Georg Solti (New York: Alfred A. Knopf, 1997).

Jason Stearns. Photograph courtesy of Neil Funkhouser Artists Management.

Thomas Stewart. Photograph by Iain Scott.

Jeffery Swann. Photograph by James Kriegsmann.

Anthony Tommasini. "Richard Wagner, Musical Mensch" by Anthony Tommasini, *New York Times*, April 10, 2005. Copyright © The New York Times Co. Reprinted with permission.

Arturo Toscanini. From *Toscanini* by Harvey Sachs (Philadelphia and New York: J. B. Lippincott, 1978) and *The Letters of Arturo Toscanini* by Arturo Toscanini, edited and translated by Harvey Sachs (New York: Alfred A. Knopf, 2002).

Astrid Varnay. From *55 Years in Five Acts: My Life in Opera* by Astrid Varnay with Donald Arthur (Boston: Northeastern University Press, 2000).

Paul Verlaine. "Parsifal" by Paul Verlaine, www. monsalvat.com.

Shirley Verrett. From *I Never Walked Alone* by Shirley Verrett (New York: Wiley, 2003). Photograph by Milton Feinberg.

Richard Wagner. *From My Life* by Richard Wagner, translated by Andrew Gray (New York: Da Capo Press, 1983). *The Assumption of the Virgin* by Titian, courtesy of Basilica Santa Maria Gloriosa dei Frari, Venice.

John Ward. Photograph courtesy of Welsh National Opera.

Virginia Woolf. From *Virginia Woolf by* James King (New York: W. W. Norton, 1995).

Epilogue. From *Ernest Newman: A Memoir* by Vera Newman (New York: Alfred A. Knopf, 1964).